BALANCED BODY

BALANCED BODY

THE BODY CENTER WORKOUT PROGRAM FOR MEN

DONALD CHARLES RICHARDSON

PHOTOGRAPHS BY ALBERT BRAY

Exercise movements and routines created or correlated by William Buckingham, Director, New York Body Center

Styling and Grooming by Christopher Welles
Activewear by Henry Grethel
Design by Ken Sansone

Harmony Books/New York

Publisher's Note: This book includes exercise instructions and an exercise program for the reader to follow. However, not all exercises are designed for all individuals. Before starting these or any other exercises or exercise program you should consult your doctor for advice.

Published by Harmony Books, a division of Crown Publishers, Inc., One Park Avenue, New York, New York 10016, and simultaneously in Canada by General Publishing Company Limited

HARMONY and colophon are trademarks of Crown Publishers, Inc.

Manufactured in the United States of America

Library of Congress Cataloging in Publication Data
Richardson, Donald Charles.
The balanced body.

1. Exercise for men. I. Body Center. II. Title.
GV482.5.R52   1984   613.7′044   84-3801
ISBN 0-517-55497-6

10 9 8 7 6 5 4 3 2

First Edition

To Peter Simon, senior editor,
and the staff of Gentlemen's Quarterly
for the opportunities
they have consistently provided

CONTENTS

INTRODUCTION

The Balanced Life

The Balanced Body Program for men is a comprehensive series of fitness routines devised by the Body Center in response to individual needs and goals. It is an honest and realistic approach to fitness that will reflect your own personal style; a fitness program designed to bring your body into line with the rest of your life and help you maintain it. The word *balance* in the name of the program is central to the entire concept: balance between muscle groups; balance in the comparative size of body parts; balance in everyday life.

Intelligent and involved men in the 1980s have a variety of interests and concerns: business, social, professional. It is foolish to suggest, as some fitness authorities have in the past, that a man should adopt an exercise routine requiring a greater commitment than that given to any other pursuit. On the other hand, it is clearly not possible to accomplish significant fitness goals with little or no effort. But there *is* a middle ground. The Body Center Program views a man's fitness experience as one aspect of life that is equal to, but not more important than, his other interests and goals.

Today, more than ever, it is important that your body work with you. You need to be in good shape to withstand the business and social pressures that have become commonplace in our lives. Looking your best is an asset that has never been more important. The constantly increasing emphasis on an athletic appearance as a sign of good health has made a commitment to fitness a requirement in many business situations.

But it is not only in response to external pressures that you need to look your very best. The internal sense of well-being and self-esteem that you achieve by success in your fitness goals is truly elating. Your self-confidence will be reflected in your approach to the other aspects of your life, thus creating a positive cycle of accomplishment.

The positive cycle is an integral part of the Body Center Program. We are all aware of behavioral snowballing. If you are overweight and out of shape, it is simpler to continue eating and avoiding exercise than to change your habits. But the opposite is also true: The better you look, the more you accomplish, and the greater your productivity—the more you want to look good, accomplish, and produce.

The most difficult part of any new venture is taking the first step forward. Many of us, fearing failure, are reluctant to make the attempt. It is vital, however, that you realize you control your own body, and if you make and fulfill your commitment to your goals, *it is not possible to fail.* Not only can you reach your own physical potential, but you will be able to bring your body up to the current standard of male physical perfection.

Male Physiques: Then and Now

In the past, the standard of men's physical attractiveness, usually based on the physiques of a few prominent figures, was an unobtainable goal for many men. For example, in the 1950s, following World War II, the ideal American male was substantial in build. His large and heavy frame reflected postwar prosperity; his physique was a statement of

success. Big was equated with healthy. There are men today who are still battling the eating habits they learned as children during this period.

Then, in the 1960s, a dramatic change took place. Suddenly, men, influenced by college students, began shedding their excess pounds. Social and political activism did not seem to go with a well-fed appearance. The body of the male in the 1960s did a total about-face. Thin, at times almost emaciated, the young men of America led the way to the slender body. Like it or not, the emphasis on youth during that time required that the rest of the male population follow. The gaunt look was further encouraged by the culture heroes of the day. Rock stars and folk singers such as Mick Jagger and Jimi Hendrix displayed painfully thin forms that became the keynote for physical style. Unfortunately, this look was a difficult achievement for many and totally impossible for others.

But as the turbulent times began to settle and the 1970s dawned, the thin look was replaced by a physique even more difficult to achieve. With the emergence in the new decade of bodybuilders such as Arnold Schwarzenegger and Franco Columbo, the fashionable physique underwent another complete change. Suddenly men wanted to be muscular—not heavy, as in the 1950s, but beefy with bulging arms and striking chests. And if the thin, formless look of the 1960s required dietary dedication, the bodybuilder bulk of the 1970s demanded a full-time commitment.

Creating a large, bodybuilder physique is not only difficult to achieve but a major responsibility to maintain. The 1970s found men facing an interest that threatened to take over their lives. This awkward combination of a difficult goal with an onerous workout schedule left the average man of the 1970s often defeated before he had even begun exercising. It is not surprising that many men did not accomplish their goals.

However, the exercise issue was to become even more complex. The constantly increasing interest in the fitness aspects of exercise, combined with the growing popularity of all sorts of exercise, gave rise to numerous conflicting systems, methods, and philosophies that would confuse even the most knowledgeable exercise enthusiast. The average man of the 1970s valiantly attempted to sift through the astonishing number of programs, routines, procedures, claims, counterclaims, and directions in an attempt to settle on a workable and viable approach to fitness that would provide him with the good looking and athletic body he was trying to achieve.

Moreover, some training philosophies have been based on self-defeating body stereotyping. Much has been written about the three basic body types: *mesomorph,* a large frame with good muscle-building potential; *endomorph,* bulky, with a tendency to overweight; and *ectomorph,* thin, with difficulty increasing muscle size. In reality, there are as many body types as there are bodies. Some men have well-developed shoulders, whereas their legs are small and undersize. This situation would imply that an individual has a mesomorphic upper body and an ectomorphic lower body—a circumstance that is confusing at best and senseless at worst. If a man places his body into one of the classifications, he automatically accepts the limitations and parameters that the classification implies and thus creates a self-defeating situation at the very start of his exercise program. Your body is an entity in itself and, as such, has its own characteristics, of which you as a mature, intelligent man should be aware.

Even if a man found exercises that suited him, he still could often fall into a training trap. For example, he might concentrate on muscle groups that responded well, working them almost exclusively in the hope that their development would detract attention from his undertrained muscles. Or he might attempt muscular compensation by exercising his entire body with equal

stress and force, contributing to his overall development but, unfortunately, maintaining the discrepancy inherent in his muscle groups.

The overall confusion of techniques,

goals, and philosophies during this period of time resulted in a variety of counterproductive situations. Some men switched programs and routines often, searching for the best, and achieving partial success, or none at all, with each method. Sometimes men found that their bodies were in no better shape after exercise than before. This unfortunate circumstance contributed to the ease with which many men dropped out of exercise programs.

It was during these confusing times that the Body Centers first opened. Their membership rapidly established itself as a cross section of American males, with businessmen and professional people joining students and younger men. However, another group of men who selected the Body Center for their fitness needs had a direct influence on the creation of the Body Center Program. Many models, dancers, and actors began coming to the Body Centers to train. For these men, fitness and looking good were integral aspects of their lives—and their livelihood. They wanted and needed a routine that would be commensurate with a busy life-style and a need to look their best. These men needed to achieve and maintain a natural, well-balanced, all-American look that reflected their personal and professional goals. It was a natural extension of this premise that led to the Body

Center's conclusion that all men, regardless of their profession, had a similar need for an exercise program to help them look their individual best.

The concept was supported in the late 1970s and early 1980s by the changes in the fashionable physique. The new movement was not as dramatic as in the prior two decades. The new look reflects men's interest in a simpler style, a more natural physical appearance. In fact, it is almost as if the two extremes—the bodybuilder's bulk and the gaunt man's slightness—have coalesced into the best of both worlds. The American male recognized, as the ancient Greeks had, that a man's body looks its best when the natural structure is emphasized and the muscle groups are symmetrically in balance with one another. For each man the dimensions will be different, but the proportions will be the same. For the first time, it is possible for every man to reach a physical goal that is his very own. The look of the 1980s became, and still is, a reflection of a man's personal and individual interest in his appearance and his concern about fitness.

The physical look of the 1980s is not a mass-produced appearance. One man's body is not a duplicate of someone else's but an individual statement of his own very best look. Size and muscle are not imposed on a man's frame. Rather, the basic inherent qualities of natural muscles, definition, and proportion should be drawn from his particular structure. When these three attributes are brought to their highest level, the result is a visually attractive and fit physique that is a functional asset to a man's other life goals.

The Body Center Program was created to aid each man in his quest for his own personal peak potential, his own *symmetry*, "beauty of form arising from balanced proportions" (Webster's 7th).

Using the mirror as your guide, with supplemental measuring formulas based on the dimension of wrist and waist, you will discover your own *ideal* state of symmetry and proportion. With this information you then will create your individual program, basing it on the needs of your own structure. You will adapt and choose movements from the innovative weight-resistance exercises that have been selected or created for optimum results in slimming, toning, or building. These exercises are combined with aerobics and stretches to promote your accomplishments and ensure whole-body participation in the fitness process.

The fundamental in-gym routine described here is based on a three-day in-gym week. It requires seventy-five minutes to complete each workout, or a little more than the average lunch hour. Additional routines are designed to handle special body situations and individual concerns while supplementing the in-gym workout.

This program will help you discover your own ideal look, while increasing your strength, stamina, and general fitness.

The Mature Body

The Balanced Body Program is as useful for older men as it is for younger men. Fitness, exercise, and looking good do not end at age twenty-five. Since the mid-1960s we have been immersed in a youth culture. However, the same group that created this situation, the members of the post–World War II baby boom, are growing up. Today they are between the ages of thirty-five and forty. These men want to look good, and many of them have exercised sporadically since their early youth.

If fitness has not been a priority in your life before now, however, there is no reason you cannot begin a program to make you look and feel better, regardless of your age.

If you are a mature man who has not exercised before, the medical checkup is especially important. Do not attempt any exercise program until you have thoroughly investigated your basic physical health.

Many mature men are concerned about the initial stress or strain that they might encounter as they start an exercise program. Obviously, if you have not worked out before, the enthusiasm that you take to your first workout can be reflected in sore muscles. The only way to avoid this situation is to begin your program slowly, being careful not to overextend your body and possibly cause injury. To this end, the program recommends a special stretching routine to precede your regular in-gym routine (see page 50).

For men over forty, many of whom are at the peak of their professional responsibilities, the time spent exercising can be especially worthwhile. A man's performance in business will be vastly improved if he is at his physical peak. Moreover, a man who values himself cannot afford *not* to exercise. The cardiovascular and overall health benefits of exercise make it increasingly important as one grows older.

Some mature men resist going to the gym because they think that their good looks are a thing of the past, that great bodies belong to the young. Or they feel intimidated by the younger men working out near them, reasoning that they cannot duplicate the accomplishments of the younger members. These thoughts are absolute nonsense. In the first place, every man, regardless of his current age, had to begin sometime. And youth does not automatically guarantee an excellently toned physique. There are a great many younger men who have neglected their bodies.

On the other hand, physical changes in the body cause muscular strength and endurance to reach their peak usually in a man's early thirties. This means that while a man of forty and a man of twenty may start with the same muscular potential, the younger man's ability will grow as the older man's declines. However, *the mature man has strengths that he probably did not have in his youth.* He knows himself better than does a younger man. He has made inroads into his career, established himself professionally, and settled into a life-style. He has the willpower to honor commitments and follow through on goals he sets for himself. He knows his strengths and his weaknesses and how to use one to compensate for the other.

All these attributes are invaluable in the training process. The age barrrier has been broken many times by athletes and average men alike. If you are in good health and have been thoroughly checked by your doctor, there is no reason why you cannot do the Body Center Program by using your superior will power, self-knowledge, and maturity to assist you in reaching your goals.

Your Balanced Body

No matter what your age, the Body Center Program cannot promise to give you a great body—no program can. It is your body that you are working with, and the accomplishments, achievements, and successes reflected in your physique are yours. The Body Center has provided the instructions, movements, and formulas. The fulfillment of the program is up to you. *But you can succeed.* With concentration, dedication, and objectivity, you will see and feel a difference in just a few weeks, as each workout brings you closer to your own physical potential—your own balanced body.

chapter one

HOW THE BODY CENTER PROGRAM WORKS

Balance and Symmetry

A balanced body is one in which all the muscle groups are in symmetrical proportion to one another. For example, ideally, your calf and upper arm (triceps and biceps) should be of equal size; your abdominal area, including your stomach and sides (rectus abdominus and oblique muscles), should be approximately twice the size of your upper arm; your chest should be 8 to 10 inches larger than your abdominal area; your hips and buttocks should be 5 to 7 inches larger than your waist; your shoulders should be 6 to 8 inches larger than your chest; your thigh should be 7 inches larger than your calf.

The establishment of your own symmetrical parameters will be based on your individual physique. Using formulas adapted and created by the Body Center, you will learn to slim, build, or tone every major muscle group in your body until you achieve the balance and proportion inherent in your own body. In other words, you will practice a unique kind of body sculpture.

Most men have one or more muscle group that responds easily to exercise, developing rapidly, and showing considerable results in a short time. Other muscle groups can take longer to grow or achieve definition. Some individuals have muscle groups that appear to be resistant to exercise, remaining in a constant state of underdevelopment.

It is difficult to generalize about these differences in men and muscle. One example of this situation is the chest area. Many men find that their chest muscles respond quickly to exercise, simply because this muscle group is often large. However, these same men may find it more difficult to increase the size or definition of their leg or arm muscles.

Even the most well-developed bodies have areas of special concern, and it is up to each man to deal with his difficult muscle groups appropriately. In the Body Center Program you will learn how to support, define, and build your weaker muscle groups as you train and maintain your strong areas.

All men have some physique problem. You may think that your situation is insurmountable, but you will be surprised by what dedication to the Body Center Program can accomplish. In the program, no muscle group is prominent, no area is underdeveloped.

The Program

The two most innovative aspects of the Body Center Program are the placement and extent of the stretching movements and the selective weight-resistance exercises.

In most programs that include weight-resistance movements, stretches are placed at the beginning of the routine and completed before the weight-resistance training begins. Consequently, it is possible that the last muscles to be exercised can contract and lose much of the value of the initial warm-up. In the Body Center Program, each muscle group is warmed up with stretching movements immediately before the weight-resistance training for that area is begun, thus fully preparing the muscle for the stress of the weight-resistance exercise. This procedure not only reduces the chance of sore or stiff muscles but also contributes to dexterity and strength.

The second innovation is the use of *selective* weight-resistance movements.

There are two standard precepts upon which weight-resistance exercise is founded: (1) there are particular exer-

cises for each muscle group; and (2) heavy weight and few repetitions will build the muscle, and light weight and many repetitions will tone and define the muscle. However, these precepts can be extended. The actual movement of the weight can contribute to the growth, toning, or even slenderizing of a particular area of the body. An essential premise upon which the Body Center Program is based is that weight-resistance exercises that fully contract a muscle and limit extension will *build;* exercises that both contract and extend the muscle fully will *tone;* and exercises that extend the muscle and limit contraction are best for *slimming.*

Maintaining the premise of heavy weight for building, and light weight for toning and slimming, the Body Center has correlated and created weight-resistance movements in which the action and direction of the exercise is geared to your building, toning, or slimming goals. With each exercise is included the appropriate amount of weight to use and the most advantageous number of repetitions.

As your body responds to the program, you can adjust your exercises to the needs of your muscles. If one area grows quickly and moves out of proportion to the rest of your body, you can change to the toning exercises. If one muscle group is undersize, you can add bulk and size with the building movements.

The entire program is adjustable and tailored to your individual needs. It is based on a 3-day in-gym week, 75 minutes per workout.

For simplicity, the program divides the body into seven body parts, exercising the major muscle in each part:

1. **Legs** (gastrocnemius and quadriceps)

2. **Buttocks and Hips** (gluteus maximus)

3. **Stomach and Sides** (rectus abdominis and obliquus externus abdominis)

4. **Back** (latissimus dorsi and erector spinae)

5. **Chest** (pectoralis major)

6. **Shoulders** (deltoids)

7. **Arms** (biceps and triceps)

Complete instructions for each movement and aspect of the program are listed with each muscle-group section.

The Basic Routine

The basic in-gym routine is divided into four sections, as follows:

1. The warm-up. Completed in 5 minutes, the warm-up employs either a bicycle or a treadmill to ease the body into the exercise experience. The warm-up is suitable for all body types and should be completed before any workout.

2. Stretches. There is a two-part stretch for each muscle group, suitable for all body types. The stretches are *held* for 30 seconds each, avoiding the "bounce" motion that can pull muscles.

3. Weight-resistance exercises. There are three weight-resistance exercises for each muscle group: *building,* for muscle groups that are undersize according to your body-symmetry calculations; *toning,* for muscle groups that are the right size and need only to be maintained, tightened, or defined; *slimming,* for those areas of your body that are too large according to your balanced body parameters.

4. Aerobic toning. This is a 15-minute, 3-phase routine designed to release the stress created by the weight-resistance training, to tone the body as a whole, and to supply a cardiovascular workout.

Chapter Three of this book provides instructions and advice about planning your own balanced body program. Then you will find a series of routines for both in-gym exercise (Chapters Four–Five) and exercise away from the gym (Chapter Six). All the routines are directed toward the concept of a balanced body, and all the exercises in the routines are designed to either support or expand the basic in-gym program.

Chapter Seven discusses nutrition and diet.

An intriguing aspect of the interest in exercise is that the primary purpose for which most men go to the gym—*to look good*—is actually secondary in importance to the need for exercise—*better health.* Very few men exercise to improve their cardiovascular systems; they want to look good. With the Body Center Program you can look your best, mold your physique into its most functional shape for your life-style, and attain the health benefits provided by a good workout as well.

The program does not depend on anyone else. Your goals, your achievements, your rewards are your own accomplishments. Recognizing your own worth is often cited as a benefit of strenuous exercise—reaching that little bit farther, striving for that small extra gain. With the Body Center Program, not only will you learn to appreciate your own abilities and strengths, but your body will reflect your decision to present your best to the world.

chapter two

PREPARING FOR EXERCISE

Have a Medical Examination

Before beginning any exercise program, your first consideration should be your initial state of fitness. Be sure to have a complete physical checkup before you begin. Your flexibility, dexterity, muscle tone, stamina, and all-around good health will help determine goals, direct the strenuousness of your program, and create the limitations under which you must begin.

Even if you are healthy, there may be certain areas of your body that must be given added consideration in exercise. For example, the lower back, due to its susceptibility to stress and strain, can become a problem if exercise affecting that section is not done carefully.

Having ascertained your limitations, if any, and your soundness for an extensive program of conditioning and physical rehabilitation, your next step is to find a fitness facility. There should be one in your area. Health clubs are becoming increasingly popular.

Choose an Exercise Facility

There are Body Center Clubs in New York, San Francisco, and Los Angeles. Each center is equipped with a varied and complete selection of machines, free weights, and other facilities. However, the Body Center Program is designed to be used in *any* fitness facility that offers basic weight-resistance and fitness equipment.

There are three important considerations to be remembered when selecting your gym or health club.

1. The first prerequisite for any fitness facility is obviously the equipment the club provides. The gym should contain adequate room and facilities for cardiovascular exercise, along with free weights, stretching mats, sauna, steam room, and clean shower area. In addition, there should be an adequate staff of instructors and other personnel to assist you and answer questions.

2. Your second consideration should be the club's availability. The location of the club and its schedule of open hours will prove to be very important aspects of your training. If you are at your best early in the morning, and your gym does not open until 10:00 A.M., you will not give a peak performance in your workout. And if after work or on your days off you find that you must travel some distance to your gym, it rapidly becomes very simple to find excuses to forego your routine. Many gyms base their finances on the premise that only a small percentage of their members will actually use the facility. It has been proven that although many men are full of enthusiasm at the beginning of their program, their interest wanes and slowly so does their attendance at the gym. Consequently, it is important that you select a club with a schedule and location that will encourage rather than retard your participation.

3. The third consideration is somewhat more personal. Each health club or gym has a distinct personality, and it is advantageous to find one that will match your own.

One of the few undeniable facts about health clubs is that there are plenty to choose from. There are clubs that stress the use of machines, others that suggest a social club, some that pride themselves on creating bodybuilders. Whatever the type of club, you will accomplish more if you are in an atmosphere of accomplishment. Look over a prospective club carefully before joining and, if possible, consider a short-term membership.

A club's personality, schedule, location, and facilities are all factors within your control and should be used to support your program rather than as excuses for defeat.

Make a Commitment

Once you have determined your ability to enter a fitness program and have selected an appropriate facility, it is time for you to make a real commitment to the exercise experience in terms of *goals, direction,* and *dedication.*

A *goal* is a primary factor in beginning and succeeding in an exercise program. It is vital that you have an accurate and realistic perception of the results you are seeking and the gains you want to achieve.

The key word in goal-setting is *realism*. Too often a man will defeat himself before he starts by setting a goal that requires extensive change in too short a time and may even require a totally different basic physical structure than the one he possesses. To set a goal beyond your ability is counterproductive and self-defeating.

The men pictured in this book have attained their goals. Some of the men are professional models, others are students or businessmen. They range in age from nineteen to forty-one and represent a wide variety of body "types." Some of the men have large basic structures, others are very slim; but they each have an individual framework within which they must work. As you study the movements pictured, do not attempt to duplicate any one model's physique. You are your own person and your body has as much individual potential as those pictured. Your goal must reflect your own potential.

Direction is the method or means you use to accomplish your goals. Unfortunately, at present there are nearly as many fitness methods as there are fitness experts, and it is not easy to sort through the various approaches.

Many of the popular exercise programs are based on one of these three concepts: a particular piece of equipment; a certain routine; or an individual's personal methods. Restricting yourself to one type of equipment is not only unnecessary in the diverse fitness world, but it can limit your accomplishment. It can also be very boring. Following another individual's program will also limit your personal growth. Even more absurd are the photocopied collections of standardized movements passed out by some health clubs to all members upon joining. How one set of exercises can achieve optimum results for every individual is a problem with which you, fortunately, do not have to deal.

In the last few years, personal training has gained popularity. The one-on-one workout can be very helpful, but personal training also has its drawbacks. Aside from the cost, which can be prohibitive, if you relinquish control of your fitness progress to someone else, you may cease to take any responsibility for your own progress. Regardless of how dedicated (or how expensive) your trainer may be, no one can possibly have as great an interest in your accomplishments as you do yourself.

Dedication and self-knowledge are constant, recurring themes of the Body Center Program. You must have not only a full and complete awareness of your physical structure and potential, along with your individual physical weak points and less responsive muscle groups, but you need to be able to recognize your emotional strengths and weaknesses as well. Learn about your excuse system—that series of manufactured reasons you employ when you don't want to do something. Learn to recognize the signals that indicate you are growing bored with a particular experience. Then become acquainted with a variety of exercises that will accomplish the same goals, and continue your physical development. Take the time to discover where your strengths lie, and learn to redirect your strength of mind to those aspects of your exercise routine that you often overlook or don't enjoy doing.

The Body Center Program is a carefully orchestrated collection of movements that will, with your energy and dedication, provide you with the look that best represents you. Learning about yourself is the first step in learning how the Body Center Program works for you.

Evaluate Your Body

Learning about your physical body and your individual muscle groups requires *study, observation,* and *objectivity.* You must know which of your muscles need building, which need toning, and which areas of your body need slimming. The best and most obvious method to learn your physical strong points and weak points is to use the mirror.

Stand naked in front of a full-length mirror. Try to forget that you are looking at yourself and study the body facing you as if it were a stranger you have to critically judge and improve. View this stranger as your representative in the world. Is this the body you want associated with you?

Admittedly, this is a very difficult process, particularly at the start of an exercise program. Objectivity about oneself is a Herculean task. Most of us are either too kind or too harsh about ourselves. And we leave the mirror totally taken in by our self-deception or emotionally annihilated by our self-criticism. But learning objectivity is a great step forward in successfully completing an exercise program.

Do not be discouraged by your present condition—or your age. Even though the mirror will begin as your greatest critic, it can eventually be your greatest supporter. Your physical reflection is the ultimate guide to the direction, extent, and, eventually, the success of your exercise program. When you study your reflection in the mirror, keep in mind the following *ideal symmetrical physique,* and begin at the bottom of your body:

1. Calves. Your calves should be streamlined and appear similar in size to your triceps/biceps area.

2. Thighs. Your thighs should be firm, not fleshy, and continue the muscular contour of the calf.

3. Buttocks. Your buttocks and hips should be taut and slightly larger than your waist.

4. Stomach and Sides. Your stomach should be flat and well defined, with your sides (obliques) converging as a vortex in the groin and hip area.

5. Chest. Your chest should be well defined on the bottom, with muscular development in the upper part. Both sides of the chest area should be symmetrical.

6. Shoulders. Your shoulders should be the widest part of the body, the beginning of the body's taper to the hips.

7. Arms. Your arms should be strong, defined, and sinewy, the upper arms matching your calves in size, tapering down to the wrist.

Find Your Ideal Proportions

To supplement what you learn from looking in the mirror, the Body Center suggests two formulas to assist you in planning your exercise program. It is interesting to note that one of the formulas is based on what is considered one of the most static areas of the body; and the other is based on what is considered one of the most variable areas of the body.

THE WRIST FORMULA

The static area is the wrist. The concept of basing your proportions on your wrist is not new, but the Body Center has revised and expanded the basic formula to reflect the Body Center Program. The circumference of the wrist is relatively free from change, even as weight increases or decreases, or with muscular development.

It must be noted that in some cases the wrist will not be an accurate basic measurement. Some men have wrists that are unusually large or small for the rest of their body. Naturally, these men should not train their physiques to reflect a basic measurement that is not compatible with the rest of their structure. If after measuring your wrist you find that the resulting proportions are either absurdly large or small, do *not* use the wrist formula to aid you in establishing your training goals. For example, if your wrist is 6 inches in circumference, and you are over 6 feet tall, the resulting abdominal measurement based on the wrist formula of 4 to 4.25 times the wrist would mean that your stomach should be approximately 26 to 28 inches. This is obviously very small and an impossible goal for someone with a large physical frame.

An unusual wrist measurement will not affect your ability to achieve a well-proportioned body. You should base your goal on the waist formula. For the many men who can use the wrist formula, however, it can be a helpful indication of symmetrical proportion. After measuring your wrist, follow the directions on the wrist formula chart on page 34 and note the ideal dimensions for your muscle groups. For example, if your wrist measures 7 inches, your upper arm should be 14 inches, your stomach between 28 and 30 inches, your calves, 14 inches, and so on.

THE WAIST FORMULA

The other suggested formula was created by the Body Center. It is an unusual approach to symmetrical proportions because it is based on an extremely variable section of the body—the waist area. Excess weight, bad posture, a sedentary life-style, and improper exercise can all contribute to an out-of-shape abdominal area. However, the stomach muscles are the visual center of your balanced body, and a good-looking abdominal area can often compensate for many other underdeveloped muscle groups. In addition, the condition of the abdominal muscles can often indicate the care and attention that has been paid to your physique as a whole. The balanced-body stomach area should be well-defined, tight, and, ideally, flat. If you use the waist formula, you should find your ideal measurement on the waist measurement chart on page

35 based on your height and build. For example, if you are 5 feet 7 inches your ideal waist measurement should be between 28 and 30 inches. If your waist measures 28 inches, then your upper arm should be 13 inches, your calf 13 inches, your thigh 20 inches, and so on, as the chart indicates.

Take Your Measurements

The measurements for your ideal physique should be taken as indicated in the illustration on page 33. Measure your body *before your workout* in the flexed or relaxed state indicated by the figure; that is, the wrist is flat, the forearm is measured extended, the upper arm is measured flexed, the shoulders are measured straight, the chest is measured expanded, the waist is measured relaxed—under the last rib, the hips are measured across the largest part of the buttocks, the thighs are measured at the widest part, the calves are measured at the widest part, the legs are measured relaxed.

Remember, the proportions and measurements in both the charts are considered *ideal*. It is important to remember that Webster's definition of perfection includes "taking something to its greatest potential." So even if you do not have *ideal* proportions, you can have *personal perfection* by taking your body to its greatest potential. Remember to be realistic when setting your goals. Do not attempt or expect overnight results. If you are out of shape and have never exercised before, it will take a while to begin the exercise process; but with dedication you should see definite results in a few weeks and begin to feel better and look better in as little as three months.

Regardless of which formula you use as a guide in setting your goals, always remember to return to the mirror to accurately assess your body's progress.

Measure Your Body

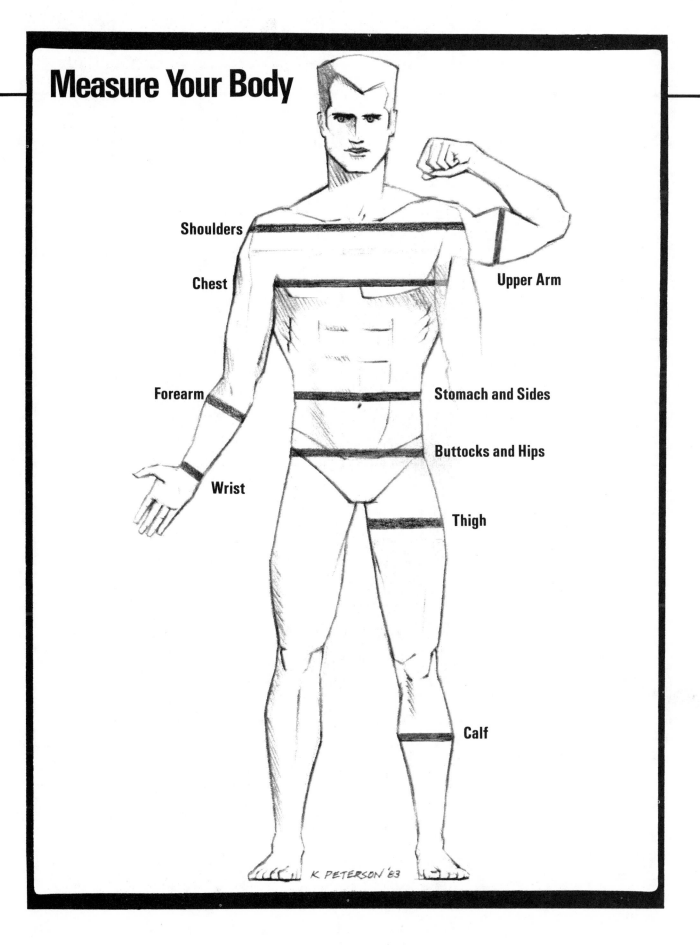

Shoulders

Chest

Upper Arm

Forearm

Stomach and Sides

Buttocks and Hips

Wrist

Thigh

Calf

K PETERSON '83

Wrist Formula Chart

BODY PART	FORMULA	IDEAL	ACTUAL
1. Wrist	Above the projecting bone	None	6 3/4"
2. Forearm	1.5 × wrist	10 1/8"	10 5/8
3. Upper Arm	2 × wrist	13.5	13.5
4. Waist	4.25–4.5 × wrist	30 3/8	36
5. Chest	8–10 inches larger than waist	40 3/8	40
6. Shoulders	5–7 inches larger than chest	47 7/8	47
7. Hips	5 inches larger than waist	35 3/8	39
8. Calves	Same as upper arm	13 1/2	16
9. Thighs	7 inches larger than calf	20 1/2	24

Waist Formula Chart

BODY PART	FORMULA	IDEAL	ACTUAL
1. Waist	Ideal from graph	32	36
2. Chest	8–10 inches larger than waist	42	40
3. Shoulders	5–7 inches larger than chest	49	47
4. Upper Arm	Half waist less 1 inch	15	13.5
5. Forearm	Half upper arm	7.5	10 5/8
6. Hips	5 inches larger than waist	37	39
7. Calves	Same as upper arm	15	16
8. Thighs	7 inches larger than calf	22	24

Ideal Waist Measurements

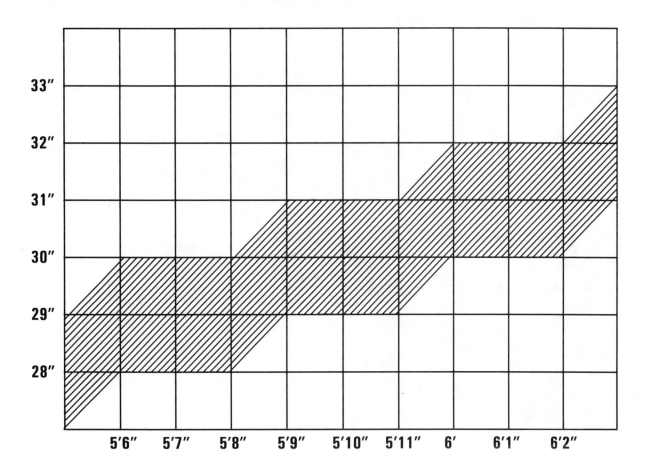

chapter three

WORKING OUT YOUR ROUTINE

After you have studied your reflection in the mirror, worked out your symmetrical guidelines using one of the proportion charts, and discovered your strong and weak physical areas, you are ready to select from Chapter Four the weight-resistance exercises that are suitable for you.

Your body will change as you proceed through your program. Consequently, periodic adjustments to your routine will be necessary. As you build your strength and endurance, you will find that a formerly weak or unresponsive muscle has begun to grow. This is exciting and encouraging, but it is more important that you do not let these newfound muscles dominate your body. Balance is always the keynote of your program. If a certain muscle group is growing out of proportion to the others, switch to the toning or slimming movements. Conversely, if an area you have been slimming or toning begins to decrease too much in size, adjust your program and do the building movements. Constant scrutiny and attention are necessary to your body and your program.

The exercises in Chapter Four have been selected because of their appropriateness for the individual muscles. However, if you are physically unable to complete the movement suggested for a particular muscle group or are without the required equipment, it will be necessary for you to find an *alternate exercise*. The Body Center Program does not restrict you to the movements in Chapter Four. Substitution is possible if you follow the one simple but essential premise upon which the Body Center Program is based: Weight-resistance exercises that fully contract a muscle and limit extension will *build;* exercises that both contract and extend the muscle fully will *tone;* and exercises that extend the area are best for *slimming*.

Slimming, Toning, and Building

This process is most easily understood by looking at the biceps section of the weight-resistance exercises. Without weights or equipment, follow the biceps exercises. For *slimming*, extend your arm down to your side. You will note that the biceps area is flat. Move your arm slightly, bending it backward, and it flattens even more. Following the instructions, curl your arm up to ¾ of a complete contraction. As your arm travels up through the curl, you will see that, having begun in the extended position, the muscle begins the building contraction only at the ¾ point. Consequently, the movement actually works without building out the bicep area and contributes to its slimming process.

The *toning* movement instructs you to move from the fully extended position to total contraction. Extending the arm through the complete range of movement completely works the muscle, thus tightening and defining it.

For *building,* the movement begins in total contraction and the arm is lowered to ¾ of a full extension. Holding your arm in the fully contracted position and lowering it, as you follow the exercise, will demonstrate that the muscle is never completely out of contraction. The pressure is more constant and maintained. Consequently, the muscle grows.

Contraction Exercises Will Not Slim

Movements that fully contract the muscle *should never be done* for a muscle group or physical area that you are trying *to reduce.* The most obvious and notable area of the body that often falls victim to this misuse is the abdominal area.

The sit-up has become one of the staple exercise movements in many routines. And it is a good exercise, provided it is used intelligently. If done incorrectly it can cause lower-back problems. Sit-ups *do* develop strength and tighten the stomach area. However, the strengthening and developing benefits of sit-ups are liabilities for the man whose abdominal area is not flat, simply because they tighten the stomach area *as it exists.*

The balanced body stomach is flat, toned, well defined. If your physique tends toward a protuberant abdominal area, then the slimming movements will tighten and strengthen the area while aiding in flattening it as well. If your stomach muscles are in good shape but tend to develop outward, as those of many bodybuilders and athletes do, then the toning muscles will aid in pulling the area in.

Naturally, if your stomach is flat and tight, the building exercises can be used to increase strength and definition.

The overweight man is especially susceptible to the protruding stomach problem. Sit-ups or any contraction exercises are not only unwise for this man but can be *counterproductive* in the long run as, even if he loses his excess weight, he might keep his waistline.

Another contraction exercise that can present problems is the crunch sit-up. This exercise concentrates even more stress on the abdominal area than does the regular sit-up and can cause an uneven abdominal section. The three horizontal sections of the abdominal muscles should be even. However, many men who do crunches develop the top section of the muscle group so that it protrudes outward, out of proportion to the rest of the abdominal muscle. This is an unnecessary situation and can be alleviated by employing more extension and toning movements.

Variations of the crunch movement are used in Chapter Six. However, they have all been adjusted to avoid the upper-muscle-section concentration.

Your Workout Chart

Keeping in mind all that you have learned about your body and having established your goals, the next step is to actually establish your program. A workout chart on which you can mark your routine appears on page 42. (Filling out this chart can also be helpful when you are looking for a health club or gym. Keeping it handy will provide you with the information about the equipment you will need for your program as you view each potential fitness facility.)

Make Your Routine Work

Keep in mind as you start your program:

1. Have your program set before you begin your routine. It is important that you know which exercises you want to do before you start, so that you do not waste time or allow your body to cool down between exercises while you decide.

2. Never take more than 30 seconds between exercises or movements. If you have finished the stretching portion of a particular muscle group, and the equipment you need for your weight-resistance exercise is in use, *do not stand idle.* Jog in place, stretch, or return to your warm-up movements. It is vital that your body stay in the exercise experience throughout your training period.

3. Breathe deeply. This may sound simple, but many men have a tendency to hold their breath while doing difficult exercise, which only makes the exercise more difficult. Breathing keeps your body relaxed and gives you added strength. When doing weight-resistance exercises, you should breathe in as you relax and breathe out as you exert.

4. If possible, work out with a partner. In addition to the added safety provided by someone watching your weight-resistance exercises, the encouragement of another person working out with you can be very helpful in reaching your goals.

5. Do not exercise immediately after a full meal. Give your body time to digest your food before beginning your routine. However, it is a good idea to eat something within an hour after you have completed your workout.

6. Ask questions. Do not be afraid to ask the staff or management of your gym about your workout. If you have specific questions about the use of certain equipment, it is wise to have it fully explained before you begin working out. You have paid to use your gym. Take advantage of it.

7. Never sacrifice form in a weight-resistance exercise for increased weight. Each weight-resistance exercise given here is followed by the suggested amount of weight to be used in the movement. However, if you find at the start of your program, or anywhere throughout it, that the weight suggested is too heavy for you to handle, move to a lighter weight until your strength increases. Form is the most important part of any weight-resistance movement, and you run the risk of counterproductive exercising, to say nothing of possible injury, if you attempt to manipulate more weight than you are capable of.

It should be noted that it is possible to cheat in virtually any weight-resistance exercise. By adjusting the position of your grip, stance, or body, you can make most exercises easier to accomplish. Unless specifically instructed, weights should never be returned to the resting position during a set. This naturally

Workout Chart

MUSCLE GROUP	STARTING MEASUREMENTS	ROUTINE (CHECK ONE)		EQUIPMENT
Calves		slimming		
		toning		
		building		
Thighs		slimming		
		toning		
		building		
Hips/Buttocks		slimming		
		toning		
		building		
Stomach (abdominals)		slimming		
		toning		
		building		
Sides (obliques)		slimming		
		toning		
		building		
Back		slimming		
		toning		
		building		
Chest		slimming		
		toning		
		building		
Shoulders		slimming		
		toning		
		building		
Front (biceps)		slimming		
		toning		
		building		
Back (triceps)		slimming		
		toning		
		building		

43

WEIGHT	SERIES	ONE-MONTH MEASUREMENTS	THREE-MONTH MEASUREMENTS	SIX-MONTH MEASUREMENTS

negates the value of the movement. If you cheat in the exercises, it will show on your physique.

8. Check your measurements once a month. Watch your body in the mirror every day as you work out. Be critical, honest, but sensitive with yourself during your mirror examinations.

9. Avoid conversation. Visit with friends later. You must keep your concentration on your workout.

10. Reach a little more each day. Robert Browning wrote that "a man's reach should exceed his grasp." This is never more true than in an exercise program. Extend your body a little further each time you lift a weight or perform a stretching movement.

11. Wear the right clothes. Some exercise authorities suggest that you should not be concerned with what you wear to exercise. Others suggest heavy sweat clothes. And some even advocate wearing nothing at all—a somewhat inappropriate suggestion for a public gym. Regardless of which idea you subscribe to, what you wear should be comfortable, functional, and encouraging. Many men can work out in shabby clothes and feel great. But if old gym clothes depress you, then it might be worth your while to find something that will make you feel good and give you a better self-image. You need to watch yourself in the mirror constantly during your routine, and your concentration should not be disturbed by your workout apparel. If it makes you feel better to wear good-looking workout clothes, then wear them. But don't restrict your program for fear that you will lose the crease in your sweat pants or get dirt on your T-shirt. You are at the gym to work!

12. Forget about exercise when you've finished. Go out and have fun. The Body Center Program is a part of your life, not all of it. Concentrate on your body during your routine, then take your mind off exercise.

Take Charge of Yourself

An exercise routine is one of the few endeavors that you can control. Your progress and achievements are the result of your decisions and dedication to the exercise experience. Regardless of the fact that achievement is dependent on the amount of effort expended in an exercise routine, every man, particularly at the beginning of his program, wonders how long it will take to reach his goals.

Naturally, the time frame depends on the extent of your goals. Any program that promises quick results, particularly one that assures you of easy and sweatless workouts, should be suspect. A great body is not an overnight accomplishment. Do not set a certain date by which you expect to have achieved your goals. Instead, choose several dates for evaluation and determination of your program. Do not forget that while what you have accomplished is vital to your self-esteem, what you *should* accomplish is important to your overall goals.

You will notice dramatic results in your body in about three months if you attack your program with dedication and enthusiasm. This is based on at least 3 workouts a week on alternate days. You may see results even sooner, depending on your goals. But it is important to remember that *exercise is a part of your life*. This means that it will always be an aspect of your life-style. The object is not to reach a certain level of performance or proportion and then stop. The final function of exercise is to help you look and feel the best you can all through your life.

chapter four

BASIC IN-GYM PROGRAM

Warm-up and Stretch

A warm-up is vital before beginning your workout. It is necessary to prepare your body for the exercise experience. Your heart and circulatory system should be *led* into your workout and stimulated to respond to your demands.

A long warm-up is not required. *Five minutes* of the following aerobic warm-up will usually be enough to begin your body's entrance into the fitness process.

Using either an exercise bicycle or treadmill, begin slowly and accelerate your speed until you reach optimum rate. Optimum rate is usually calculated by taking the maximum rate at which your heart should beat during exercise (220 beats per minute) and subtracting your age. This number is then multi-plied by the degree of effort expended during the workout.

The bicycle or treadmill you use for the warm-up will have a control that will indicate the amount of effort expended. For example, if you are 25 years old, subtract 25 from 220. Your optimum rate is 195. Working at 70-percent effort, your heart will beat 136 beats per minute; at 75-percent effort, 146 beats; and at 80-percent effort (the usual amount and the figure recommended by many fitness authorities), 156 beats per minute. Work up to this level gradually. (If your fitness facility does not have either a bike or treadmill, either jog in place or do jumping jacks for the allotted time, checking your pulse on your wrist, counting the beats.)

50

STRETCH ROUTINE FOR MEN OVER FORTY

To aid the mature individual, or someone who has not exercised regularly, the Body Center suggests a simple series of stretches that will contribute to flexibility and dexterity. This short routine is not necessary if you have been exercising before or do not suffer stiffness in any of the areas trained, but these movements can help avoid muscular stiffness. These stretches should be done immediately after your warm-up and before the leg stretches that begin your actual routine. They should also be done with the special routines you use.

In addition, these are also excellent early-morning movements to help get each day started.

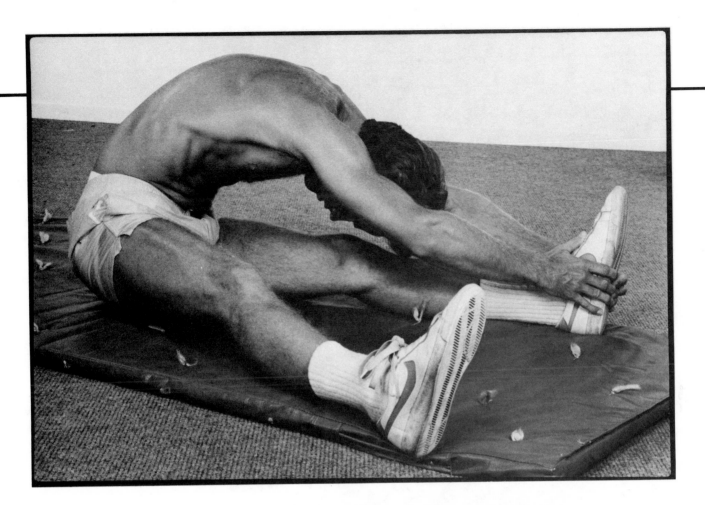

HAMSTRING STRETCH

■ Seated on the floor or an exercise mat, extend your legs flat on the floor in front of you.

■ Separate your legs, forming a V.

■ Reach forward, bending your torso, and grasp the sole of your right foot with both hands. Hold for 30 seconds and release gently.

■ Lift your upper body back to the upright position. Then bend and repeat the movement, grasping your left foot.

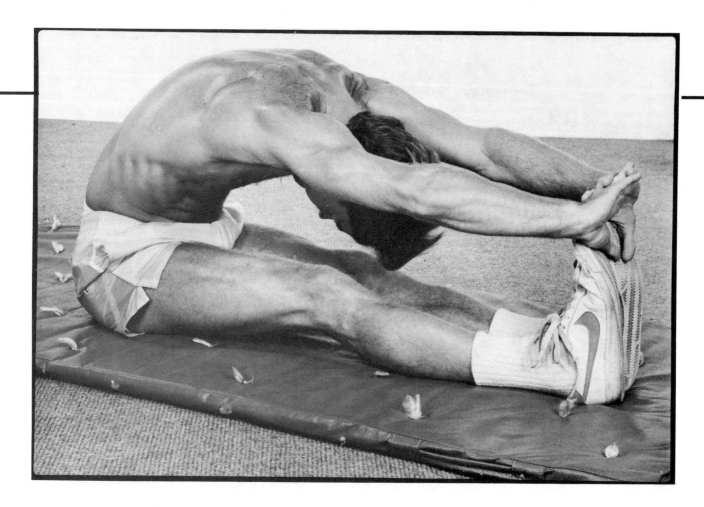

SHOULDER STRETCH

■ Seated on the floor or an exercise mat, extend your legs straight out in front of you, toes up.

■ Intertwine your fingers and bend your torso forward, arms outstretched, positioning your hands, palms out, on the bottoms of your feet.

■ Push out with your feet. Hold for 30 seconds and release gently.

LOWER BACK STRETCH

■ Lie on your back on the floor or an exercise mat. With your legs together, bring your knees to your chest.

■ Position your arms, hands clasped, behind your knees.

■ Pull your body together. Hold for 30 seconds and release gently.

Legs

Some men consider the leg muscles the most difficult to improve. Strong, muscular legs are vital to your all-around training and conditioning. Much of the stress involved in weight training is placed on the legs. In addition, your entire personal presentation suffers if your legs are not strong. In reality, your legs are capable of meeting much higher demands than you place on them in your average daily life.

The major calf muscle (gastrocnemius) is a long, slim muscle and can be difficult to build, but it will respond if you stay with it.

The major frontal thigh muscles are generally grouped together as the quadriceps. This is one of the largest muscle groups in the body and is capable of great strength.

In general, leg exercise is some of the hardest work you will have to do. The leg muscles are not always easy to sculpt to your specifications, but with concentration and dedication you can create the leg muscles you want. One added aspect of leg exercise, difficult though it is, is the excellent feeling of conditioning that you can experience throughout your whole body.

The weight-resistance exercises for the legs are divided into two sections: calves and thighs. The stretching movements for both these areas and suitable for all body types, regardless of what weight-resistance exercise is selected.

56

STRETCHES

■ Kneeling on an exercise mat, lean your upper body back, resting your buttocks on your heels, using your hands for support behind you.

■ Bend your elbows to create a stretch in the upper leg. Hold the position for 30 seconds.

■ Gently release the stretch and move to the second position.

■ Form a V with your body, placing your hands and toes on the mat, and your buttocks/lower back at the highest point.

■ Lower the heels of your feet toward a flatfooted position, concentrating the stretch in the calf area. Hold for 30 seconds and gently release.

WEIGHT-RESISTANCE EXERCISES

Calves

slimming SLANTED CALF RAISE

EQUIPMENT: Standing incline board, barbell
WEIGHT: 15 to 30 pounds
SERIES: 3 sets of 25 repetitions

■ With a barbell resting on your shoulders behind your head, balanced by your hands, position the balls and toes of your feet on the edge of the foot-rest of a standing incline board, facing in. Rest your upper body on the board. Adjust the barbell until it is as comfortable as possible; the weight is intended to accentuate the calf movement.

■ Lower your heels down to the floor as far as possible.

■ Return your heels only to the point of neutral stress. Never raise your heels to contract the calf muscle.

toning
SINGLE-LEG CALF RAISE

EQUIPMENT: 6- to 8-inch block, dumbbell

WEIGHT: 25 to 50 pounds

SERIES: 3 sets of 15 repetitions for each leg; alternate sets

■ Place a cinder block or wood block, 6 to 8 inches high, next to a wall, column, or other support.

■ Holding a dumbbell in your left hand, place the ball of the left foot on the edge of the block.

■ Position the right foot behind the left calf. Place your right hand against the support for balance.

■ Lower your left heel as far as possible toward the floor, and in one continuous movement bring the left heel up as far as possible.

■ Repeat the movements for the right calf, switching the weight to the right hand and maintaining your balance with your left hand. Complete the sets alternately.

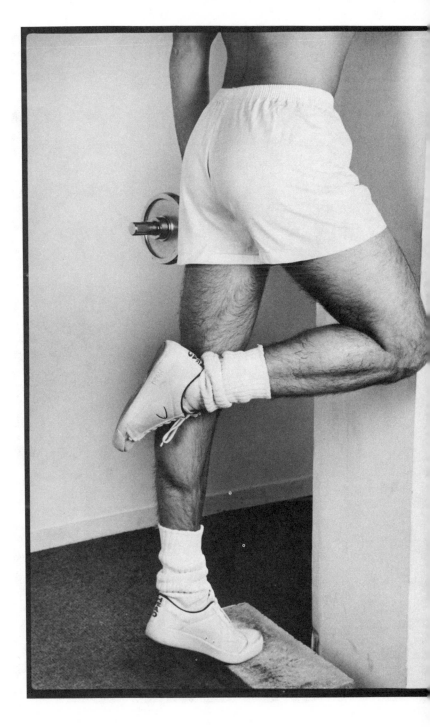

building SEEATED BARBELL CALF RAISE

EQUIPMENT: Bench, barbell
WEIGHT: 50 to 100 pounds
SERIES: 3 sets of 10 repetitions; one set in each position

■ Sit on the edge of a flat bench. Position a barbell across your knees. Place your feet together, flat on the floor. In this exercise your feet move to a different position for each set, but they must remain together and flat on the floor in all three positions.

■ *Position 1,* your feet are slightly under the seat or bench.

■ *Position 2,* your feet are even with the forward edge of the bench.

■ *Positon 3,* your feet are approximately 8 inches in front of the bench.

■ Raise your heels as far as possible and lower them slowly to the floor.

Thighs

slimming
WEIGHTED THIGH PULL

EQUIPMENT: Mat, dumbbell
WEIGHT: 10 to 20 pounds
SERIES: 3 sets of 20 repetitions

■ Kneeling on a mat, sit back on your legs. Hold a dumbbell with both hands close to your chest.

■ Slowly lean back to a 45-degree angle, then return to the upright position. Do not allow knees to leave the mat.

toning
THREE-POSITION BARBELL SQUAT

EQUIPMENT: Barbell
WEIGHT: 20 to 60 pounds
SERIES: 3 sets of 10 repetitions

■ To achieve maximum results, this exercise is done with the feet in three positions.

■ Grasp a barbell with crossed hands and position it on your shoulders in front of your neck distributing the weight comfortably.

■ Complete one set of the exercise with your feet in each of the following positions: Feet parallel, 6 inches apart, toes forward; heels together, toes pointed outward; heels apart, toes pointed inward.

■ Bending at the knees, lower your body, continuing the movement until your buttocks are almost to the floor. Return to the standing position.

■ Be careful to avoid locking your knees in the upright position.

building STRADDLE BARBELL LIFT

EQUIPMENT: Barbell
WEIGHT: 40 to 100 pounds
SERIES: 3 sets of 10 repetitions

■ Stand astride a barbell. Place one hand in front of your legs, the other behind your body. Grasp the barbell and stand straight up, arms at full extension.

■ Keeping your arms straight at all times, bend your knees, lowering the barbell approximately 12 inches below your torso.

■ Return to a standing position. It is important to keep your back straight throughout this exercise and avoid locking your knees in the upright position.

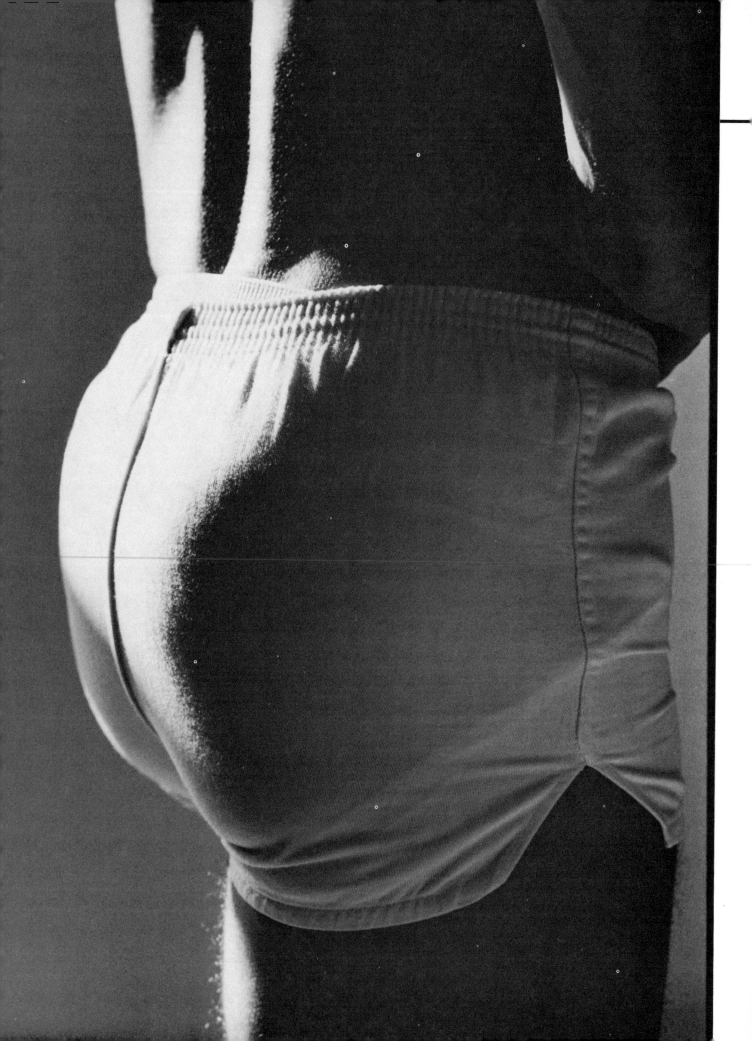

Buttocks and Hips

The buttocks muscle is wrongfully overlooked in many exercise programs. Advancing years and a sedentary life-style can cause the buttocks muscle to sag.

Not only is the buttocks muscle a vital part of a balanced body, but strong buttocks muscles (gluteus maximus) can increase the dexterity in your legs and can strengthen your lower back.

STRETCHES

■ Standing on an exercise mat, feet shoulder width apart, bend down, keeping your knees straight, and grasp your ankles.

■ Lower your upper body and head toward your legs until the stretch is felt in your buttocks. Hold for 30 seconds and release gently. Move to the second position.

■ Form a V with your body, positioning your hands and feet on the mat, creating an arch with your back.

■ Lift your right leg and extend it *to the side* and up as far as possible (preferably parallel to the floor). Hold for 30 seconds.

■ Repeat with your left leg. Be careful not to lift the leg toward the back. The leg must go out to the side to properly stretch the hips and buttocks.

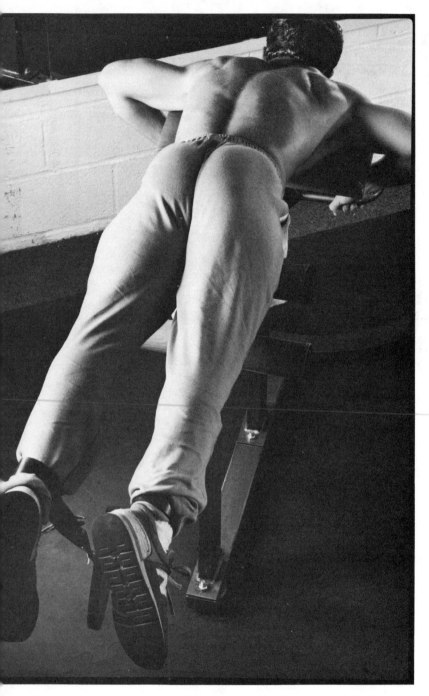

WEIGHT-RESISTANCE EXERCISES

slimming HYPEREXTENSION WEIGHTED LEG RAISE

EQUIPMENT: Hyperextension, weight plate with strap or dumbbell, pad (optional)
WEIGHT: 10 to 20 pounds
SERIES: 3 sets of 15 repetitions

■ This exercise uses the hyperextension equipment in a slightly different manner than usual. It is helpful and more comfortable to place a pad under your abdomen.

■ Attach a strapped weight plate to your ankles or hold a dumbbell between your ankles. Facing the hyperextension, position your lower abdomen on the seat section of the equipment and grasp the foot rods with your hands.

■ Your legs are now extended out, behind the hyperextension. Lift them up until they are parallel to the floor. Do not raise your legs higher than the parallel position.

■ Lower them slowly.

toning
KNEELING DUMBBELL LIFT

EQUIPMENT: Dumbbell, mat
WEIGHT: 10 pounds
SERIES: 3 sets of 10 repetitions

■ It is very important that the fulcrum of this exercise be set in the buttocks. If you do not lean far enough forward, it becomes a shoulder exercise. If you lean too far forward, you will lose your bal-ance. It will be necessary to experiment with this exercise until you feel the stress in your buttocks.

■ Place a dumbbell directly in front of you on an exercise mat. Kneel and po-sition your buttocks approximately 2 inches above your legs.

■ Lower your upper body to form a 45-degree angle with the floor, arching your back. Extend your arms fully and grasp the dumbbell with both hands.

■ Lift the dumbbell to chest height and lower it slowly.

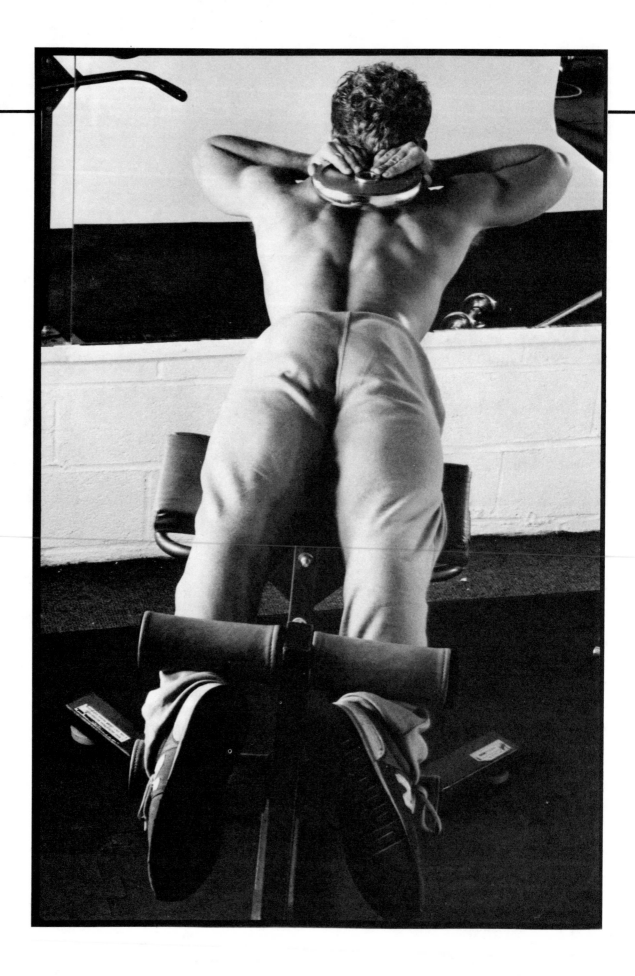

building HYPEREXTENSION BUTTOCKS CRUNCH

EQUIPMENT: Hyperextension,
weight plate or dumbbell
WEIGHT: 20 to 30 pounds
SERIES: 3 sets of 15 repetitions

■ Face down, position your stomach
on the seat of the hyperextension and
place your feet into the foot rods. Clasp
a weight plate or dumbbell with both
hands behind the neck or tightly to the
chest. Begin the movement with your
upper body parallel to the floor.

■ Raise your upper body as high as
possible and return to the parallel position. Do not allow your body to drop
below the parallel position.

Stomach and Sides

The stomach is the visual center of the body, and well-developed and strong abdominal muscles are a central and essential aspect of any good-looking body. In addition, the stomach muscles (rectus abdominis) are vital for basic movement. Without the stomach muscles it would not be possible to flex your lower back. Consequently, you need the stomach muscles just to get out of bed.

Obliques, the muscles on the sides of the abdominal area (obliquus externus abdominis) aid in the movement of the vertebral column and can be a difficult area to train properly. Excess weight around this area, or love handles, can often be found on men regardless of whether they are overweight.

Even if your love handles cannot be eliminated, this area can be strengthened and tightened. If you have a hereditary or structural predisposition to love handles, turn this problem into an asset of your balanced body by toning and defining the area. Michelangelo's *David* has obvious love handles. Remember, it is important to work with your own individual physique and turn any liabilities into positive factors.

It is also important to remember when exercising the abdominal area that *no* contraction movements should be completed if you are attempting to flatten your stomach. Sit-ups and crunches are for tightening and strengthening your stomach and will not aid in flattening the abdominal area. In fact, if you are overweight or have a protruding stomach (as do many men with otherwise good bodies), contraction exercises will simply tighten the area at its present size. You should do extension exercises until you have lost weight or reduced the size of your abdominal area.

In this section, the weight-reduction exercises are divided into two sections: stomach and sides. The stretches are for both areas and can be completed by any body type, regardless of which weight-resistance exercise is used.

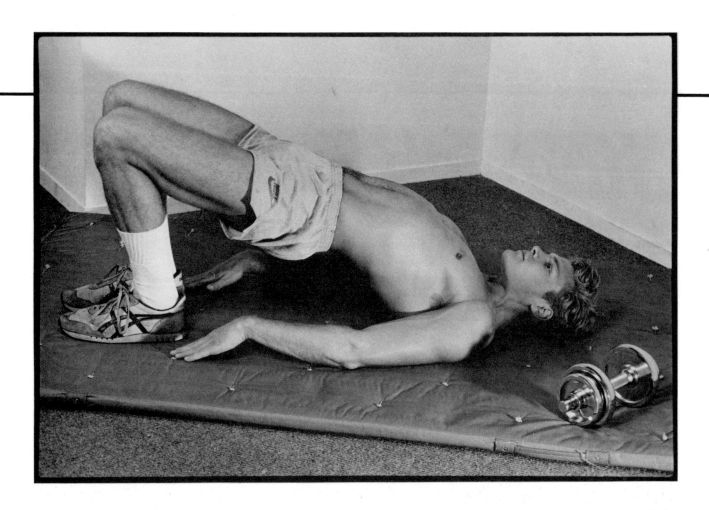

STRETCHES

■ On your back, position your shoulders and feet flat on an exercise mat, knees bent.

■ Raise your stomach as high as possible until a stretch is felt in your midsection. Hold for 30 seconds and release gently.

■ Lying on your back, raise your legs to a vertical position. Keep your legs straight.

■ Bend at the waist and bring your
legs forward to a parallel position with
the floor, your feet beyond your head.

■ Rotating with the hips as an axis,
turn your legs to the right until you feel
a stretch in the oblique area. Hold for
30 seconds and release gently.

■ Turn your legs to the left until you
feel a stretch in the oblique section.
Hold for 30 seconds and release gently.

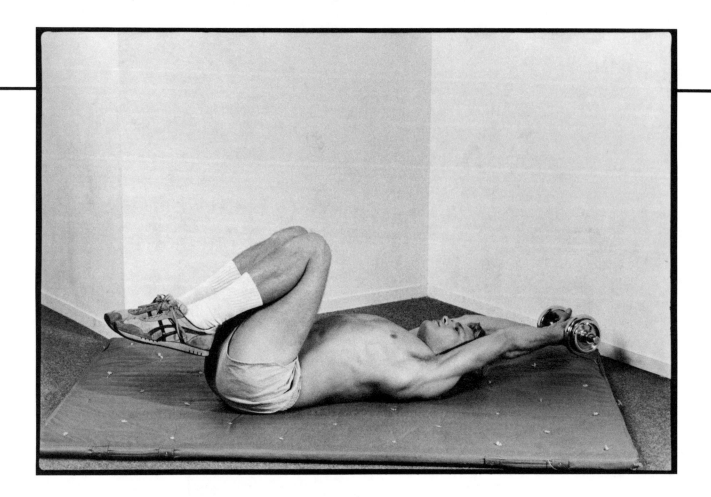

WEIGHT-RESISTANCE EXERCISES

Stomach

slimming
WEIGHTED LEG THRUST

EQUIPMENT: Dumbbell, mat
WEIGHT: 10 to 15 pounds
SERIES: 4 sets of 25 repetitions

■ Place a dumbbell behind you on a mat. Lie flat on your back and extend your arms fully behind your head. Grasp the dumbbell with both hands.

■ Lift the dumbbell approximately 2 inches from the floor and hold it in that position.

■ Bring your knees up to your chest and thrust your legs straight out, parallel to the floor, with a rapid, straight motion. Return knees to lifted position.

toning
SLANTED WEIGHTED LEG LIFT

EQUIPMENT: Slant board, weight
plate or dumbbell, pad (optional)
WEIGHT: 10 to 15 pounds
SERIES: 3 sets of 25 repetitions

■ Be very careful. Depending on your
structure, you may not be able to raise
your legs the full 24 inches, or you may
be able to raise them higher. Stay
within your point of balance or the
weight can slip from its position. A pad
placed under the weight can make this
exercise more comfortable.

■ Set a slant board at medium height.
Place a weight plate or dumbbell on
your ankles. Lie flat, face up, with your
head at the top of the board.

■ Grasp the bar or support above your
head with both hands. Raise your legs
approximately 24 inches and return
them slowly to the board.

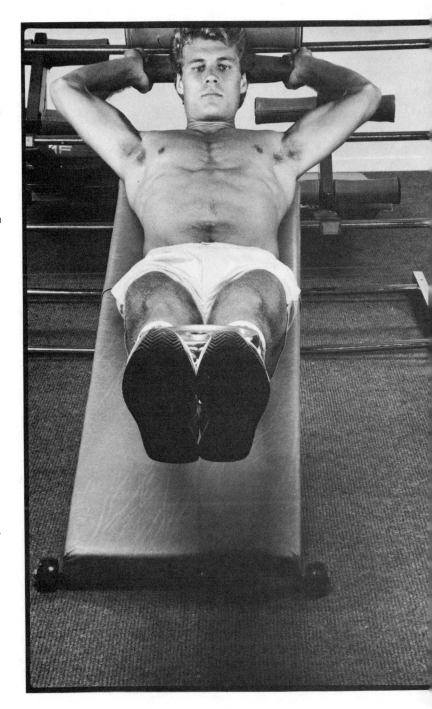

building
STANDING INCLINE FORWARD BEND

EQUIPMENT: Standing incline board, barbell
WEIGHT: 40 to 75 pounds
SERIES: 3 sets of 15 repetitions

■ Position a barbell behind your head, resting on your shoulders, held with both hands. Mount a standing incline board, face up.

■ Lean back against the board, with feet firmly placed on the footrests.

■ Lean forward at the waist, keeping your head up, attempting to touch your chest to your thighs.

■ Slowly return to the slanted upright position. Keep your back straight throughout the movement. It is important to keep the focus of the movement on the abdominal area.

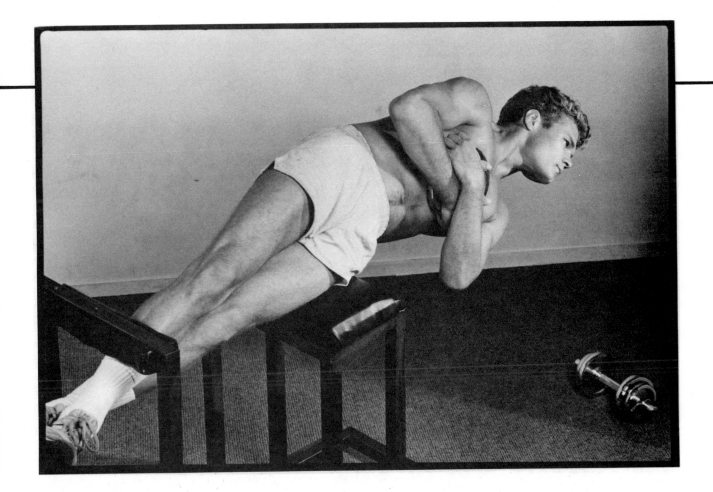

Sides

slimming HYPEREXTENSION WEIGHTED LATERAL LIFT

EQUIPMENT: Hyperextension, weight plate
WEIGHT: 10 to 25 pounds
SERIES: 3 sets of 15 repetitions for each side

■ Position your right hip on the seat of the hyperextension. Secure your feet under the foot rods. Hold a weight plate to your chest with both hands.

■ Begin the movement with your body parallel to the floor.

■ Lower your upper torso as far as possible to the floor and slowly return to the parallel position. Do not raise your torso higher than the parallel position.

■ Reverse your body and complete the movement for your left side. Complete the sets alternately.

toning
LATERAL WEIGHTED LEG LIFT

EQUIPMENT: Flat bench, weight plate with strap, or dumbbell
WEIGHT: 10 to 15 pounds
SERIES: 3 sets of 15 repetitions for each side

■ Attach a weight plate to your ankles, or hold a dumbbell between your ankles. Lying on your left side, position your upper body on a flat bench. Your left hip should be just at the edge of the bench, your legs hanging over the end.

■ Using your oblique muscle as an axis, keep your legs together and raise them as high as possible.

■ Slowly lower your legs until your feet touch the floor.

■ Reverse your body and complete the movement for your left side. Complete the sets alternately.

building
45-DEGREE WEIGHTED HYPEREXTENSION CRUNCH

EQUIPMENT: Hyperextension, weight plate
WEIGHT: 10 to 35 pounds
SERIES: 3 sets of 10 repetitions for each side

■ Position your left hip on the seat of a hyperextension. Secure your feet under the foot rods. Hold a weight plate to your chest with both hands.

■ Begin the movement with your body parallel to the floor.

■ Raise your torso as high as possible, attempting to create a 45-degree angle with the rest of your body.

■ Lower your torso slowly to the parallel position. Do not allow your torso to go lower than the parallel position.

■ Reverse your body and repeat for the right side. Complete the sets alternately.

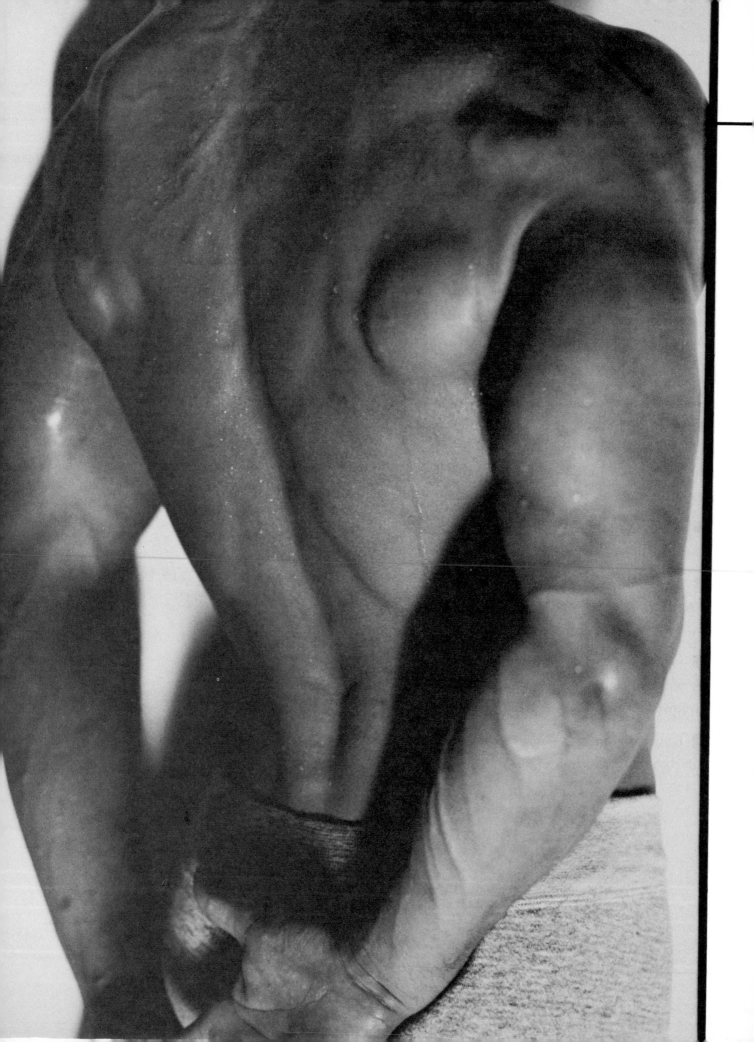

s e c t i o n 5

Back

Many weight lifters maintain that you can only be as strong as your back. Particularly when you are standing, it is true that your back functions in a supportive capacity in many weight-resistance movements for other body parts.

This additional strain on the back increases the need for specialized back exercises to keep the area in good shape.

In addition, the back muscles can be a good-looking part of your balanced body. The most visible back muscles are the ones that come down from the armpits on either side (latissimus dorsi). These muscles add extension to the chest measurement and add to the V shape on your upper torso.

There is another muscle group, not as visible, which is more important from a fitness aspect. The two columns of muscles along either side of the spine (erector spinae) are essential to the strength and health of the back and are often overlooked because they are not visibly dominant.

Both these muscle groups are trained in the weight-resistance exercises: the latissimus dorsi for strength and appearance; the erector spinae to increase the overall fitness of the back.

Exercises for the lower back can be found in Chapter Six, Section 1, Weak Areas.

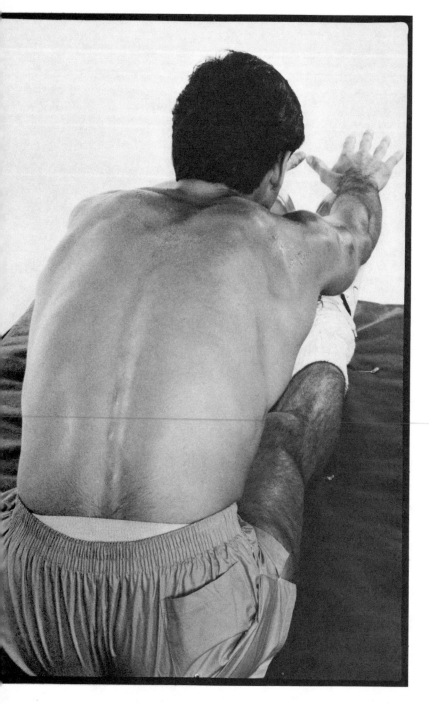

STRETCHES

■ Sit on an exercise mat with your legs straight out in front of you.

■ Bend at your waist and extend your hands straight out as far as possible, keeping your arms parallel to your legs, until a stretch is felt in your lower back. Hold for 30 seconds and release gently.

■ Remain seated and extend your arms above your head.

■ Bend your arms at the elbows and grasp the triceps area of your right arm with your left hand. (You can rest your right hand on your left elbow.)

■ Pull toward your body with your left hand as you push away from your body with your right arm, until you feel a stretch in the latissimus area. Hold for 30 seconds and release gently.

■ Switch arms and repeat the stretch for your other side.

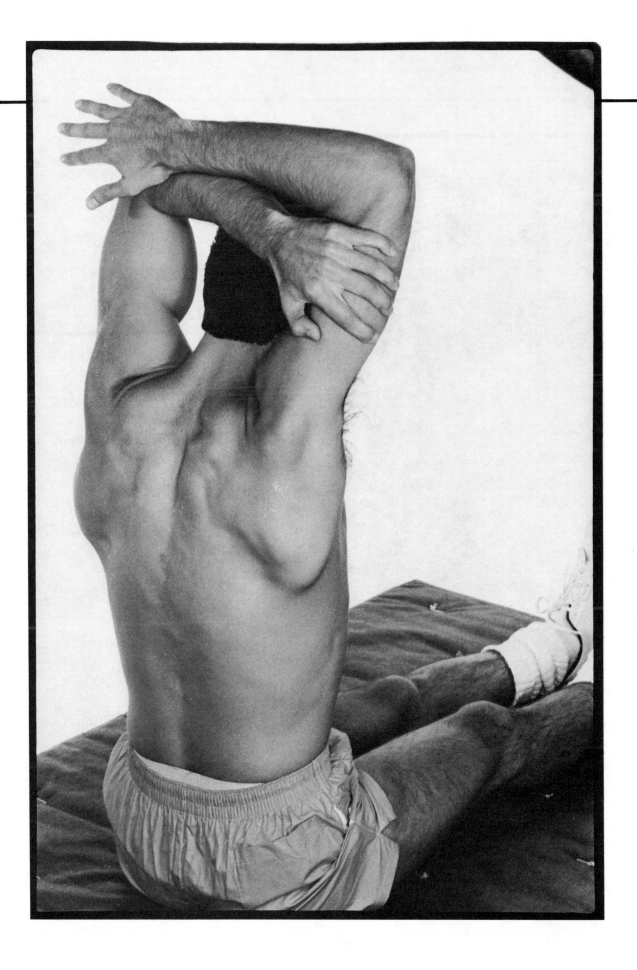

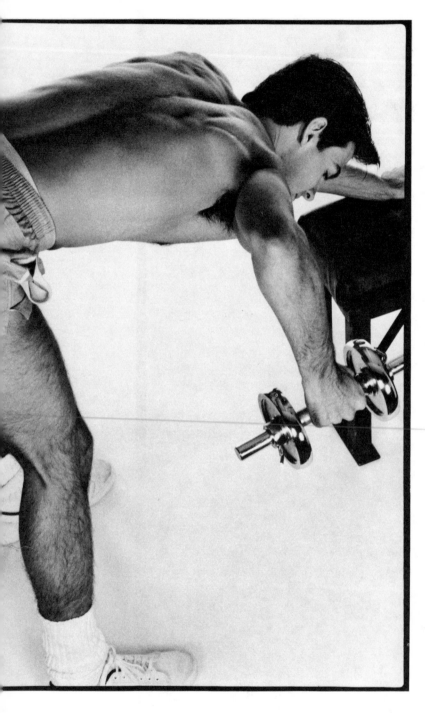

WEIGHT-RESISTANCE EXERCISES

slimming CROSS BENTOVER DUMBBELL PULL

EQUIPMENT: Dumbbell, flat bench
WEIGHT: 10 to 45 pounds
SERIES: 3 sets of 25 repetitions for each side

■ Stand with your feet planted firmly, wide apart. Place a dumbbell in front of your left foot. Lean over and rest your left hand on the edge of a flat bench.

■ Keeping your back straight, twisting your torso slightly, pick up the dumbbell with your right hand.

■ Bring your right arm up, bending the elbow, until your arm is level with your body.

■ Return to the starting position, but do not allow the weight to touch the floor between repetitions.

■ Alternate sets for each side.

toning
HYPEREXTENSION DUMBBELL PULL-UP

EQUIPMENT: Hyperextension, 2
dumbbells, pad (optional)

WEIGHT: 10 to 45 pounds on each
dumbbell

SERIES: 3 sets of 10 repetitions

■ You may find that a pad under the
stomach area will increase comfort.

■ Place two dumbbells on the floor,
one on either side of a hyperextension.
Position your body, face down, on the
hyperextension. Place your feet se-
curely in the foot rods.

■ Extend your arms straight down to
the floor and grasp the dumbbells.

■ Bending your elbows, bring your
arms straight up until the weights are
level with your torso.

■ Return your arms to the fully extended downward position.

88

building
CHINNING BAR WEIGHTED PULL-UP

EQUIPMENT: Chinning bar, weight plate with strap, or dumbbell
WEIGHT: 5 to 25 pounds
SERIES: 3 sets of 10 repetitions; one set in each hand position

■ To maximize participation of the back muscles, this exercise is done in three positions.

■ Attach a weight plate with a strap to your ankles, or hold a dumbbell between your ankles.

■ Grasp a chinning bar firmly with both hands, palms out.

■ For the first set, place your hands at your widest possible grasp.

■ Bring your body up until the bar is level with your neck. Make sure that your head is in front of the bar. Return to ¾ extension.

■ For the second set, place your hands shoulder-width.

■ Bring your body up until the bar is level with your neck. Make sure that your head is in front of the bar. Return to ¾ extension.

■ For the third set, place your hands only 3 inches apart.

■ Bring your body up until the bar is level with your neck. Make sure that your head is in front of the bar. Return to ¾ extension.

■ Do not reach full downward extension during a set.

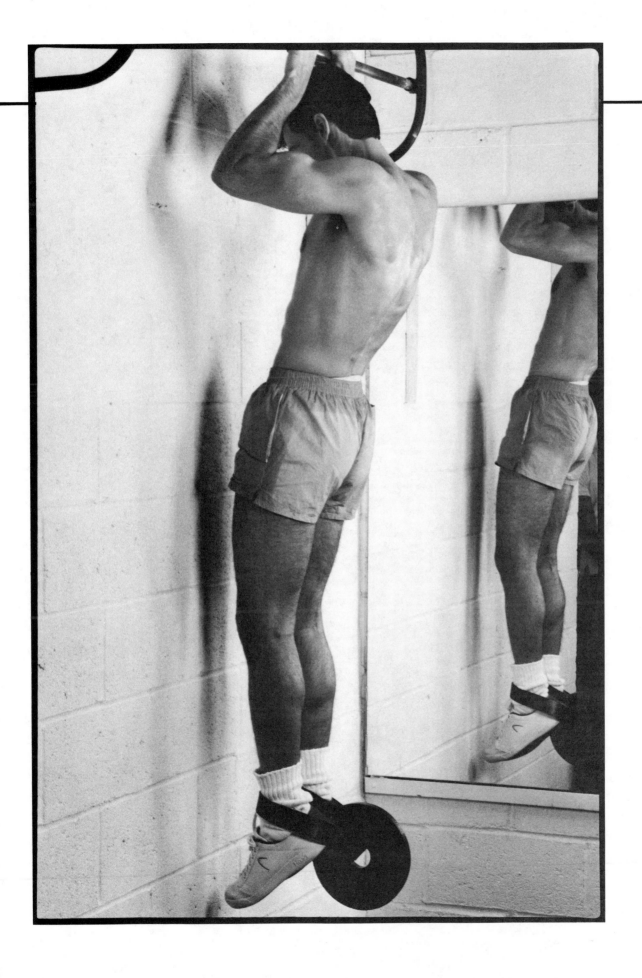

section 6

Chest

The muscle of the chest (pectoralis major) is one of the largest and most easily developed muscles in the body. The chest area in most men readily responds to exercise. This circumstance, which can be very positive, can also act against your balanced body if the chest is allowed to develop out of proportion to the rest of your physique.

To be properly developed, your chest should be exercised from three points: above, center, and below. This diverse action will help sculpt the chest area and add definition and shape.

The three-point training can be achieved by adjusting the position of your body. In all three of the weight-resistance exercises that follow, the three-point training is accomplished by employing three different bench positions which place the body at the correct angles.

One position has been used to demonstrate each movement.

STRETCHES

■ Seated on an exercise mat, position
your arms behind you and interlock
your fingers or grasp one hand with the
other.

■ Push outward with your hands.
Hold for 30 seconds and release gently.

■ Lift your arms above your head and
intertwine your fingers, positioning
your palms up.

■ Push with your hands. Hold for 30
seconds and release gently.

WEIGHT-RESISTANCE EXERCISES

slimming PULLOVER

EQUIPMENT: Dumbbell, flat bench, incline bench, decline bench
WEIGHT: 15 to 30 pounds
SERIES: 3 sets of 20 repetitions; one set in each position

■ Place a dumbbell on the floor at the head of a flat bench. Lie on your back on the bench.

■ Extend your arms above your head to the floor and grasp the dumbbell with both hands.

■ Bending your elbows slightly, pull the dumbbell over your head down to your chest.

■ Return to the extended position, lowering the dumbbell as far to the floor as possible without actually touching. Complete one set on the flat bench.

■ Repeat the exercise on both the decline and incline benches.

toning
FLYS

EQUIPMENT: 2 dumbbells, flat bench, incline bench, decline bench
WEIGHT: 15 to 25 pounds each
SERIES: 3 sets of 10 repetitions; one set in each position

■ Holding a dumbbell in each hand, lie on your back on a flat bench.

■ Begin the movement with both arms straight up, perpendicular to your body.

■ With elbows slightly bent, lower your arms fully extended, out to the sides, continuing the movement as far toward the floor as possible without actually touching.

■ Return your arms to the upright position.

■ Complete one set each on the flat bench, decline bench, and incline bench.

building PRESSES

EQUIPMENT: Barbell, flat bench, incline bench, decline bench
WEIGHT: 45 to 150 pounds
SERIES: 3 sets of 10 repetitions; one set in each position

■ Lie on your back on a flat bench. Grasp a barbell firmly with both hands. Adjust your grip until your elbows are perpendicular to the floor and your upper arms parallel to the bar.

■ Begin the movement with your arms fully extended, perpendicular to your body.

■ Lower the barbell to one inch above your chest, then extend your arms straight up, taking care not to lock your elbows in the fully extended position.

■ Complete one set on the flat bench, one set on the decline bench, and one set on the incline bench.

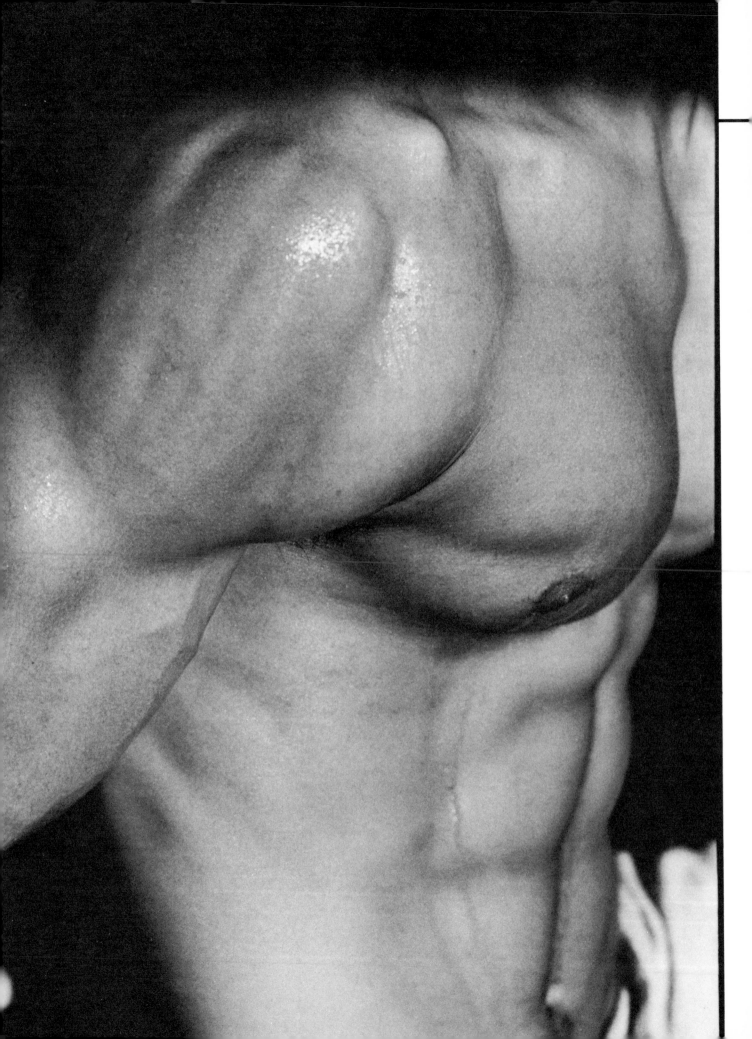

Shoulders

Strong, well-built shoulders are an important part of your balanced body. The shoulders, visually the top muscle group, create the initial point of the V taper of your upper torso. Also, as the muscles at the top of the arms, the shoulders (deltoids) must be balanced with your arms and must be strong to aid in arm development.

The shoulder muscles are divided into three sections: anterior—the front of the shoulder; lateral—the side of the shoulder; posterior—the rear of the shoulder. For proper development, all three of these areas must be trained. Consequently, there are three movements in each of the weight-resistance exercises. The movements remain constant in all three categories while you adjust the position of your body for each goal classification: slimming, toning, building. This procedure guarantees the involvement of all three sections of the shoulder muscles, while adhering to your individual needs.

The stretches are for use regardless of what weight-resistance position you use.

In the illustrations, one movement is demonstrated for each position.

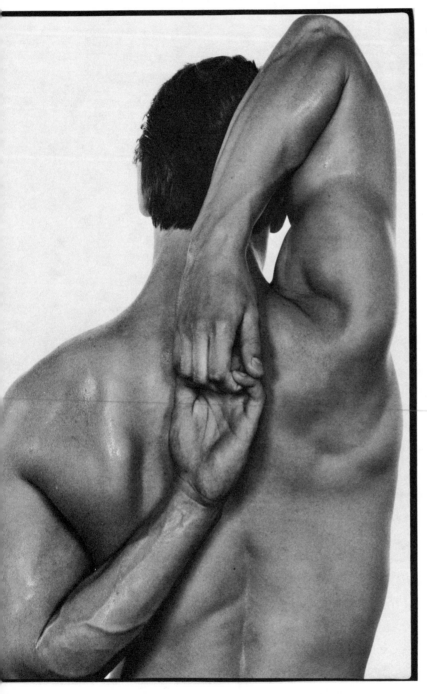

STRETCHES

■ Kneel on an exercise mat.

■ Position your left arm behind your back from the bottom, with your elbow bent.

■ Extend your right arm over your shoulder.

■ Clasp your hands together in the center of your back.

■ Pull. Hold for 30 seconds and release gently.

■ Extend your right arm straight up above your head while you extend your left arm straight down.

■ Push both arms out. Hold for 30 seconds and release gently.

■ Raise your left arm up as you lower your right arm.

■ Switch positions, clasping your arms behind your back again. Pull. Hold for 30 seconds and release gently.

■ Extend your left arm straight up as you extend your right arm straight down.

■ Push both arms out. Hold for 30 seconds and release gently.

WEIGHT-RESISTANCE EXERCISES

The following three movements are done in each of the weight-resistance exercises. The position of your body is altered to achieve your slimming, toning, or building goals. For *slimming,* the movements are completed on a flat bench, face down, your body positioned with your shoulders on the edge of the bench, your head extended over the edge. Keep your head up.

For *toning,* the movements are completed on a hyperextension, face down, your hips resting on the seat of the hyperextension. Keep your head up.

For *building,* the movements are completed standing, knees slightly bent, back straight, head looking straight forward. Complete the lateral lift, the frontal lift, and the backward fly with your body in the appropriate position. One position is demonstrated in each of the photographs.

LATERAL LIFT

■ Hold a dumbbell in each hand, arms fully extended but relaxed.

■ Lift your arms, elbows slightly bent, away from your body until your arms are parallel to the floor.

■ Return to the fully extended position.

FRONTAL LIFT

■ Hold a dumbbell in each hand, arms extended in a relaxed position.

■ Bend your arms at the elbows very slightly.

■ Extend your arms directly in front of you, lifting up until you reach eye level.

■ Return to starting position.

BACKWARD FLY

■ Hold a dumbbell in each hand. Bend your arms at the elbow to a 45-degree angle; your forearms should be parallel to the floor.

■ Lift your forearms until the dumbbells are at your armpits and your elbows are above your back.

■ Return to the starting position.

slimming

EQUIPMENT: 2 dumbbells, flat bench
WEIGHT: 20 pounds on each dumb-bell
SERIES: 3 sets of 20 repetitions; one set of each movement

■ Complete one set each of the lateral lift, the frontal lift, and backward fly, positioned face-down on a flat bench.

toning

EQUIPMENT: 2 dumbbells, hyperextension
WEIGHT: 15 pounds on each dumbbell
SERIES: 3 sets of 10 repetitions; one
set each movement

■ Complete one set each the lateral
lift, the frontal lift, and the backward
fly, positioned face-down on a hyperextension.

building

EQUIPMENT: 2 dumbbells
WEIGHT: 20 pounds on each dumbbell
SERIES: 3 sets of 10 repetitions; one
set of each movement

■ Complete one set each of the lateral
lift, the frontal lift, and the backward
fly, while standing, legs slightly bent,
feet apart, toes pointed straight out.

Arms

Almost every man doing weight-resistance exercise wants well-developed and strong arms. Your arms need to be trained just as the rest of your physique does. However, it should be noted that each time you lift a weight or complete any exercise in which you hold weights, your arms are receiving a certain amount of exercise. This circumstance can help add strength to your arms, and this increased strength can work either for or against you. Naturally, if you need to increase the size of your arms to be in proportion with your balanced body, the added strength is a positive factor. But if your arms are already large enough, you could fall into the trap of building your arms out of proportion to the rest of your body.

Two of the muscles that make up good-looking arms (triceps and biceps) need attention and training. Most men will find that their forearms will also respond to this training, and for additional exercises for forearms, see page 138. It is very important, particularly due to their visibility, that your arms be developed within the context of your balanced body. Huge, undefined arms do not contribute to a good appearance; but strong arms that combine dexterity with definition can be not only a handsome aspect of your balanced body but also a valuable factor in the completion of the rest of your program.

The weight-resistance exercises for the arms are divided into two sections: biceps and triceps. Stretching movements are for all, regardless of the weight-resistance exercise selected.

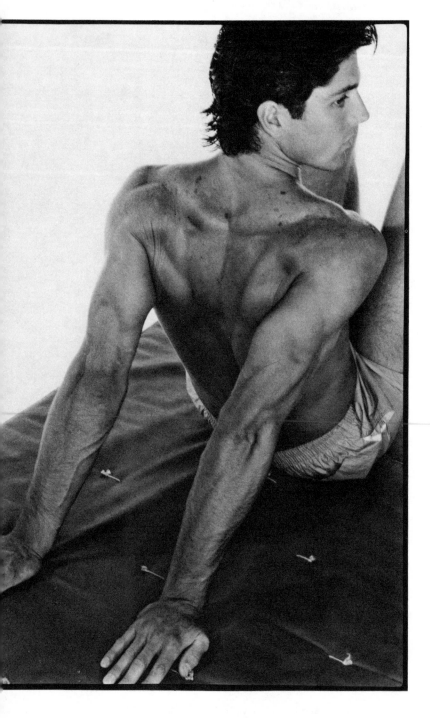

STRETCHES

■ Sit on an exercise mat, knees up, feet flat.

■ Extend your arms behind you and place your hands flat on the mat, fingers pointed out away from the body.

■ Push against your hands until a stretch is felt in your biceps. Hold for 30 seconds and release gently.

■ Reverse your hands, pointing your fingers inward toward your body.

■ Push against your hands until you feel a stretch in your triceps. Hold for 30 seconds and release gently.

WEIGHT-RESISTANCE EXERCISES

Biceps

slimming
STANDING INCLINE DUMBBELL CURL (INWARD)

EQUIPMENT: Standing incline board, 2 dumbbells
WEIGHT: 10 pounds on each dumbbell
SERIES: 3 sets of 20 repetitions for each arm

■ Holding a dumbbell in each hand, position your body face-down on a standing incline board.

■ Extend your arms fully, down toward the floor.

■ Alternately flex each arm up toward your body. Stop the curling motion when you have completed a ¾ contraction.

■ Lower each arm to the fully extended position. Remember: Do not fully contract your arm in the upward flex.

toning
STANDING INCLINE DUMBBELL CURL (OUTWARD)

EQUIPMENT: Standing incline board, 2 dumbbells
WEIGHT: 15 pounds on each dumbbell
SERIES: 3 sets of 15 repetitions for each arm

■ Holding a dumbbell in each hand, position your body face-up on a standing incline board.

■ Extend your arms fully toward the floor.

■ Alternately bring each arm up to the fully contracted position and return it to the fully extended position.

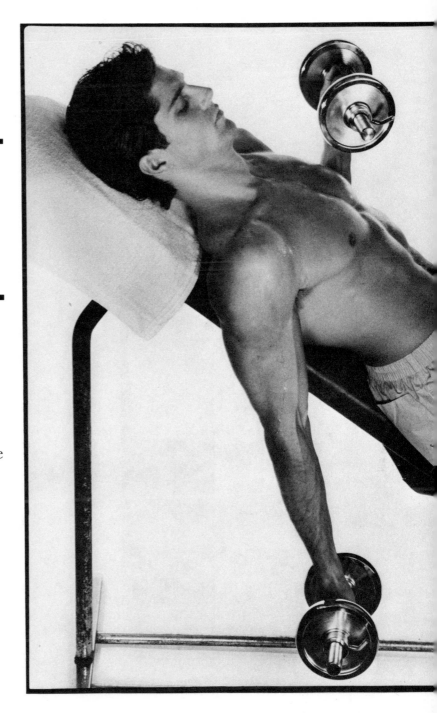

building HIGH BENCH CURL

EQUIPMENT: High flat bench, barbell
WEIGHT: 30 to 50 pounds
SERIES: 3 sets of 10 repetitions

■ Place a barbell in front of a high flat bench. (If a high flat bench is not available at your gym, you can create one by placing cinder blocks or wood blocks under any regular flat bench. The high bench must be far enough off the ground for you to extend your arms fully to the floor.) Position your body face-down on the bench. Extend your head, shoulders, and arms over the edge of the bench.

■ Keeping your head up, grasp the barbell firmly with both hands.

■ Curl your arms up, completing a full contraction.

■ Lower the barbell to ¾ of the distance to the floor. Do not fully extend your arms to the floor.

Triceps

slimming
SINGLE-ARM EXTENSION

EQUIPMENT: Dumbbell
WEIGHT: 10 pounds
SERIES: 3 sets of 20 repetitions for
each arm

■ Standing, grasp a dumbbell in your
right hand.

■ Extend your right arm directly
above your head.

■ Position your left arm behind your
head and grasp your right triceps with
your left hand.

■ Lower the dumbbell, bending only
your elbow, until the weight touches
your left shoulder.

■ Lift your arm to ¾ of the full contraction. Do not reach full contraction.

■ Reverse your arms and complete the
movement for your left triceps.

toning
WEIGHTED BENCH DIP

EQUIPMENT: 2 flat benches (one slightly higher), weight plate
WEIGHT: 10 pounds
SERIES: 3 sets of 10 repetitions

■ Position two benches, one slightly higher than the other, half your body height apart. Place a weight plate on your lap and sit on the edge of the higher bench. Place your heels on the edge of the lower bench.

■ With both hands, grasp the edge of the bench on which you are sitting.

■ Lift your body off the bench and, as you do so, slide your hands together until they are behind you.

■ Lift your body up until your arms are fully extended.

■ Lower your body toward the floor as far as possible. The movement should reach both full extension and contraction.

building
WEIGHTED REVERSE DIP

EQUIPMENT: Dip stand, weight plate
with strap, or dumbbell
WEIGHT: 10 pounds
SERIES: 3 sets of 10 repetitions

■ This exercise requires balance and
coordination. Proceed carefully.

■ Attach a weight plate with strap to
your ankles, or hold a dumbbell between your ankles.

■ Position your body on a dip stand
with your hands firmly grasping the
bars. To train the triceps, your wrists
must face out from your body, fingers
facing your body.

■ Lower your body until your forearms are parallel to the floor. Keep your
body straight.

■ Raise your body up to full upward
contraction. Do not lock your elbows at
full contraction.

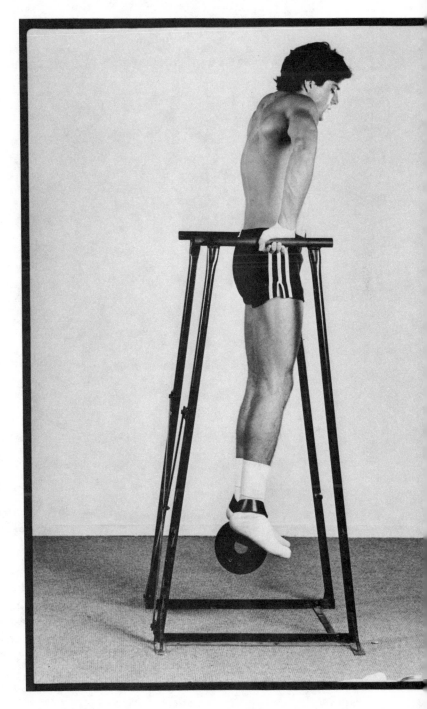

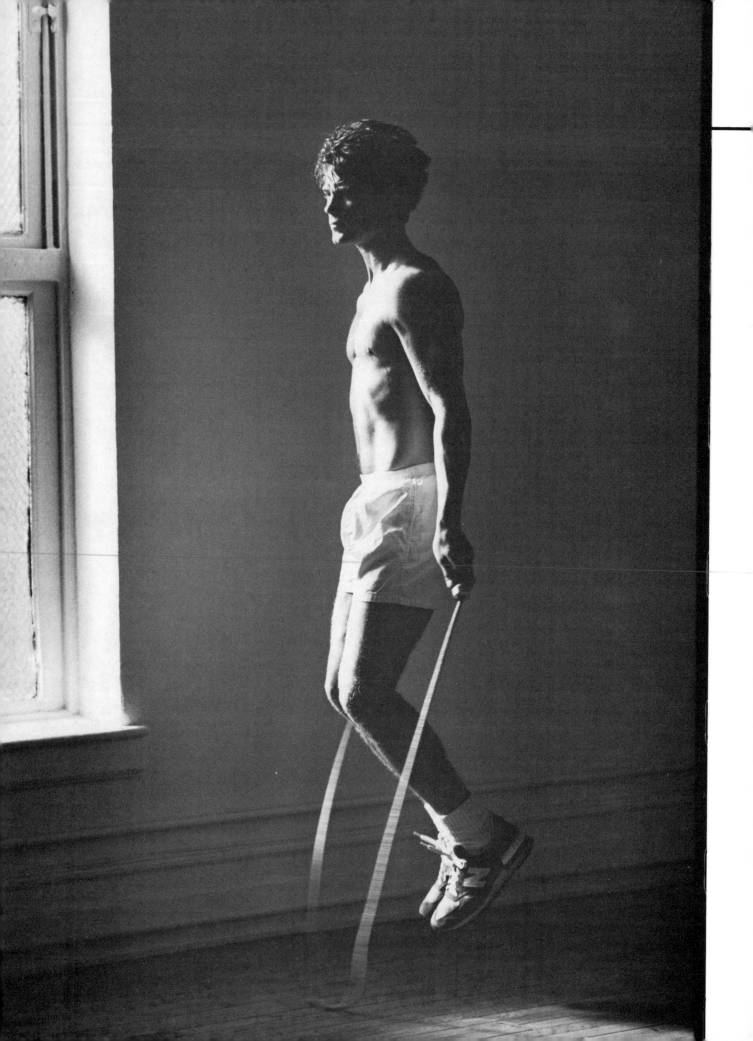

s e c t i o n   9

Aerobic Toning and Cool Down

Webster's definition of *aerobic* is "living, active . . . in the presence of oxygen." The essence of aerobic exercise is high activity, continuous exercise, and deep breathing, benefitting the heart, lungs, and cardiovascular system.

Aerobic exercises are a vital aspect of your routine; and they encourage your body sculpturing process.

In the Body Center Program, you have prepared your body for exercise with your warm-up. Then, in turn, you have prepared each muscle group for weight-resistance exercise with stretches. These stretches have loosened the muscle groups individually, adding dexterity and pliability to the muscles, thus reducing your chance of injury and encouraging your progress. But after completing your weight-resistance routine the muscles again need to be relaxed and loosened.

Weight-resistance exercises cause the blood to flow into the muscle. The "pump" that you often see after a workout is the result of the blood having rushed to the exercised muscle. Naturally, this is not a permanent condition and does not reflect actual muscle growth or strength development. Unless the pump is worked out, you can have stiff muscles. The aerobic exercise will work out the strain imposed by the weight-resistance exercises and reduce your chances of having stiff or sore muscles.

The Body Center Program is designed to bring your body to its peak both visually and *functionally*. After you have sculpted your muscles with the weight-resistance exercises, the aerobic workout will contribute to the freely functional physique.

The aerobic routine is not an adjunct to your program, but as much a part of it as the stretches and weight-resistance movements.

At the end of the aerobic routine is a cool-down period.

REBOUND

■ The aerobic routine begins with 5 minutes on the rebound unit or trampoline. Start slowly and increase your speed. If you do not have a trampoline or rebound unit, begin your aerobic routine in the same manner by jogging in place.

JUMP ROPE

■ At the end of 5 minutes, leave the rebound unit and begin jumping rope. Do not allow more than 30 seconds to pass in the period between the two activities. Begin jumping rope at the same speed at which you stopped your rebound unit exercise. Continue rope jumping for 5 minutes, maintaining your exercise rate.

JOG

■ At the end of 5 minutes of jumping rope, rest 30 seconds if necessary, and begin jogging in place. Maintain your high exercise rate for 3 or 4 minutes. Keep your knees high. Toward the end of your third minute, gradually begin to slacken your pace, gently allowing your body to come to a halt at the end of 5 minutes.

WALK

■ Now walk. Shake out your arms and legs. Stretch your body. Lean to the sides. Do not walk fast. Move at a comfortable pace around your exercise area, allowing your body a chance to cool down and relax. Breathe deeply.

chapter five

WATER WORKS!

Water is a major component of all living organisms, and your body is more than 60 percent water.

During your workout, you will lose water through perspiration, and if you are not careful, you will find that your strength will decrease due to this moisture loss. It is important that you be at top efficiency during your *entire* workout for the routine to be completely beneficial. Consequently, it is vital that you replace the water that your body loses as you sweat. Do not stop your workout and swallow great gulps of water. This can result in bloating or cramps. It is better for you to keep a container of water handy and take small sips at frequent intervals. The constant replacement of moisture will aid in maintaining a constant flow of strength, thus encouraging your performance.

Water is also a consideration after your workout. Although this is not a skin-care book, the way you treat your body after your exercise is an important aspect of your total presentation and can affect your physical goals.

The last part of your balanced body workout was the cool down. Your shower and final preparations to leave the gym are a continuation of this workout wrap-up.

Make Use of Sauna and Steam Rooms

Most health clubs now provide sauna and steam-room facilities, and the Body Center Program takes advantage of this equipment to encourage both your personal presentation and your physical progress.

Steam rooms became popular in the United States around the turn of the century. They were considered helpful in the treatment of liver disease and hangovers. Saunas, introduced later, were considered efficacious in the treatment of digestive problems. Despite the medical possibilities of the hot rooms, these facilities are used in the program for your skin and muscles.

Both sauna and steam rooms work essentially in the same manner. The heat in the rooms causes your pores to open and your sweat glands to become more active. *This increases circulation.* In addition, the blood supply to the skin is heightened, cleansing the skin. The

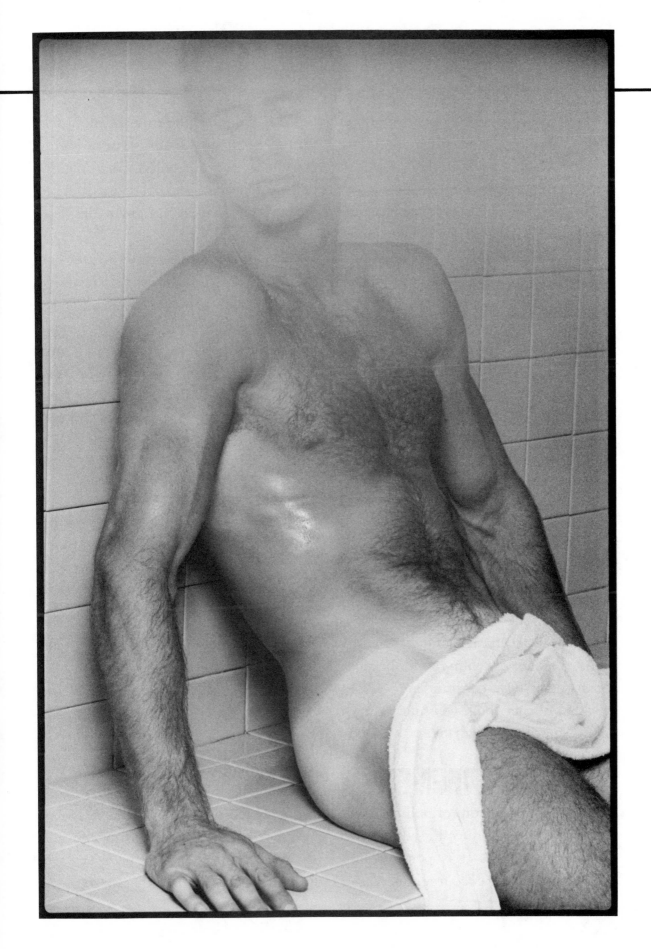

opening of your pores has two other effects: Chemicals and minerals, particularly sodium, are lost; and water is lost. Consequently, although the net effect of opening your pores can be cleansing, the final effect can be dehydration.

PLAY SAFE IN THE HOT ROOMS

There are several points to keep in mind when you use either a steam room or sauna.

You have probably seen the warning signs posted near these facilities suggesting a 30-minute time limit for their use. However, 10 minutes is really long enough in each hot room to accomplish the beneficial effects.

Elderly individuals, or people with heart disease or high blood pressure, should be particularly careful when using either of the hot rooms.

There is a greater loss of moisture in a sauna than in a steam room, because steam rooms have constant moisture in the air. In either room you may want to have water nearby to drink.

REDUCE STIFFNESS

A traditional complaint of bodybuilders is that hot rooms reduce the pump created in a workout. It is possible that because hot rooms encourage increased blood circulation, the superficial muscle pump resulting from your weight-resistance exercise will indeed slightly deflate. However, the hot rooms will not affect your actual muscular development.

Stiffness or soreness due to extensive (or improper) exercise can be a negative factor in your progress. Obviously no man wants to work out when he is sore. Your time in the hot rooms can help prevent stiff or sore muscles. Relaxing in the heat can release the strain you have imposed on your muscles and can lower your chances of being stiff.

SOFTEN SKIN

Hot rooms can provide excellent benefits for your skin. Using the steam room or sauna on a regular basis can help your skin stay young longer. Take advantage of your club's hot rooms every day you do your basic in-gym workout and it will encourage healthy skin. If your gym allows it, hot rooms are great places to shave. Your skin is softened and the shaving process is eased considerably. If shaving in your hot rooms is not permitted, you can apply your shave cream in the hot rooms and shave immediately after.

A short shower before using the hot rooms is important to remove surface dirt and sweat after your workout. A complete and thorough shower after using the hot rooms removes dead skin cells and released toxins.

After-Workout Routine

Keeping the above points in mind, the following is your after-workout routine:

Shower. A brief rinse to remove surface dirt and sweat.

Steam room. 10 minutes. Using the steam room first begins the sweating and opening of your pores slowly.

Sauna. 10 minutes.

Shave.

Final shower. Thorough soap shower to remove dead skin cells and released toxins.

Rest. Sit for 5 to 10 minutes to allow your body a chance to cool down and stop sweating.

Moisturize. To avoid dehydration of your skin, it is important to apply a moisturizer to help protect and condition your skin.

Expensive lotions and creams containing collagen or bee pollen, and such, are of no more value than simpler preparations. Your skin cannot absorb the ingredients through the pores. A moisturizer is beneficial because it stays on the surface of your skin and protects and retards loss of natural moisture.

In recent years there has been increasing concern about the use of mineral oil in many popular skin preparations. It has been suggested that mineral oil can actually combine with your body's own oils and dissolve or dry up your natural oils. To be on the safe side, try an animal fat or vegetable oil–based product. Water is a vital, simple product. Its use can contribute to your strength, stamina, and total personal presentation.

chapter six

SUPPLEMEN- TARY EXERCISE ROUTINES

This chapter of *Balanced Body* offers a series of routines for both in-gym exercise and exercise away from the gym. All the routines can be used in conjunction with the basic in-gym program, and all are directed toward the concept of a balanced body. The supplementary routines include:

1. The weak-areas-routine: designed to strengthen those areas of the body that are often weakest or most susceptible to strain or stiffness.

2. The 30-minute, in-gym toning routine: to be used when you do not have the time to complete your entire workout and want to tone your key muscle groups.

3. The at-home routine: a series of exercises selected to maintain the tone of your muscles between in-gym workouts.

4. The vacation fitness routine: to be used when you are away from any fitness facility.

5. The office antistress routine: a series of movements to reduce tension and increase stamina and productivity.

6. The 10-minute strength routine: a series of isometrics for each muscle group, valuable in increasing strength, which in turn increases your ability to expand your basic in-gym program.

These routines are offered to guarantee you the availability of some form of exercise, no matter where you are, by which you can continue your progress and maintain your accomplishments.

If you find that during a very heavy work week, for example, you have not completed your workout schedule, do not react by giving up on your program or by trying to regain any lost ground in a couple of days of extra-heavy workouts. Instead, work back into your program, and by means of these exercises go ahead with your routine. Creating and maintaining your positive cycle of accomplishment is your best guarantee of creating and maintaining your balanced body.

How and Why to Supplement Your Workout

The basic balanced-body, in-gym program is set up for a 3-day workout week, exercising alternate days for about 75 minutes. Any time you do weight-resistance exercise it is important to have a day of rest before repeating the routine. This rest period gives your muscles time to relax, respond to the exercise, and release the waste products created during your workout, which are removed by the circulatory system.

Some fitness programs are based on daily workouts. The routines in these programs exercise different muscle groups on consecutive days, avoiding repetitive, identical-muscle workouts. But in the Body Center Program, you work your entire body with weight-resistance exercise each time you complete your in-gym routine. Consequently, you need the 24-hour period away from intense repetitive movements.

This does not mean that you must avoid exercise altogether. In this section, you will find a variety of routines for use both in the gym and away from the gym, to use on rest days, on vacation, or any time you do not complete your regular routine. However, *all of these routines are compatible with the basic in-gym workout.* In fact, some of the movements can be incorporated with your in-gym routine; and some of the routines done away from the gym can add strength to your physique, which will in turn increase your ability in the basic workout.

The first two routines are to be done in the gym; the next four are for exercise away from the gym. Each routine is explained as it appears. It is important that you employ the knowledge you have gained about yourself and your body to intelligently incorporate any of these routines into your program.

Weak-Areas Routine

As you created your basic program, you learned about your weak and strong muscle groups. However, there are specific areas of your body that are generally recognized as universal weak points. These areas should be given special consideration by anyone interested in overall strength and dexterity.

The weak-areas routine can be used in two different ways:

1. As a separate workout completed on the alternate days of your basic in-gym program. If you choose to do the weak-areas routine as an individual workout, you will need to add the warm-up, appropriate stretches, and aerobic workout from your basic in-gym program to the weak-areas exercises. The correct stretching movements are listed below. For example, the abdominal stretch from your in-gym program should precede the abdominal exercises from the weak-areas routine, the buttocks stretches from the in-gym program should precede the lower back exercises from the weak-areas routine, and so on.

2. As a part of your regular in-gym workout. It is not difficult to include the weak-areas exercises in your usual workout. Simply complete the appropriate stretch indicated in the weak-areas routine, then do the weak-areas exercise and go directly to your usual weight-resistance movements for slimming, toning, or building. For example, the ankle exercise from the weak-areas routine should be inserted between the leg stretches and the calf exercises from the in-gym program. For the neck exercises, complete the shoulder stretches, then the neck exercise, followed by the weight-resistance shoulder movement of your choice, that is, for slimming, toning, or building.

WEAK AREAS: SEPARATE WORKOUT

If you elect to do the weak-areas exercises as a separate workout on the days between your basic in-gym program, the following is your routine:

Warmup (In-gym program, page 49)

Leg stretches (In-gym program, page 56)

Ankle extension on leg press (Weak Areas, page 132)

Weighted ankle flex (Weak Areas, page 132)

Buttocks stretches (In-gym program, page 67)

Standing weighted extension (Weak Areas, page 133)

Hanging oblique flex (Weak Areas, page 134)

Abdominal stretches (In-gym program, page 74)

Knee crunch (Weak Areas. For men with flat stomachs, page 135)

Scissors lift (Weak Areas. For men with protruding stomachs, page 136)

Shoulder stretches (In-gym program, page 100)

Forward neck raise (Weak Areas, page 137)

Backward neck raise (Weak Areas, page 138)

Arm stretches (In-gym program, page 108)

Wrist curl (Weak Areas, page 138)

Wrist extension (Weak Areas, page 139)

Aerobic workout (In-gym program, page 117)

AS PART OF IN-GYM PROGRAM

If you include the weak-areas exercises in your regular routine, your complete in-gym workout, including your *regular selective* weight-resistance movements from Chapter Four, will be as follows (weak-areas exercises are starred):

Warm-up (pages 50–53)

Leg stretches (pages 56–57)

*Ankle exercises (page 132)

Legs (pages 58–63)

Buttocks and hip stretches (page 67)

*Lower back exercises (pages 133–134)

Buttocks and hips (pages 68–71)

Stomach and side stretches (pages 74–75)

*Abdominal exercises (pages 135–136)

Stomach and sides (pages 76–81)

Back stretches (pages 84–85)

Back (pages 86–89)

Chest stretches (pages 92–93)

Chest (pages 94–97)

Shoulder stretches (pages 100–101)

*Neck exercises (pages 137–138)

Shoulders (pages 102–105)

Arm stretches (page 108)

*Wrist exercises (pages 138–139)

Arms (pages 109–115)

Aerobic toning (pages 118–119)

WEAK AREAS EXERCISES

Ankles

Unfortunately, ankle exercises are essentially uninteresting, but they can be very valuable. Just as your wrists need strength to aid your arms in exercise, so your ankles need strength to help support your legs. The ankle exercises are like the wrist exercises in that the most visible results of the movements are not seen on the ankles themselves, but on the front and sides of the calves. These sections of the calf muscles, when developed, can add bulk and definition to your calf muscles—a valuable training asset for men with small legs.

ANKLE EXTENSION ON LEG PRESS

EQUIPMENT: Leg press
WEIGHT: 10 pounds
SERIES: 25 repetitions

■ Position your body on a leg press, feet up. Set the leg press so that your knees are completely bent at a relaxed position.

■ Place the balls of your feet, shoulder-width apart, on the press platform.

■ Without extending your knees, press your toes forward, extending your ankles, and return to starting position.

WEIGHTED ANKLE FLEX

EQUIPMENT: Flat bench, weight plate, towel (optional)
WEIGHT: 5 pounds
SERIES: 25 repetitions for each ankle

■ A towel placed between the weight plate and your foot can increase comfort.

■ Sit on a flat bench, knees bent, feet flat on the floor. Place a weight plate atop your right foot and hold it without pressure with your hands.

■ Keeping your heel on the floor, lift the ball of your foot upward, and return it to the floor.

■ Repeat for the left ankle.

Lower Back

For many men, the lower back area is a constant concern. Lower back pain can be brought on by stress, overexertion, old injuries, or an awkward twist or turn. In Chapter Two, you were advised to consider this area before beginning any exercise program. But even if you have a healthy lower back, you should train this area for two reasons: (1) It is important to your overall fitness to keep your lower back strong and flexible; and (2) lifting, turning, and bending are all movements you make throughout your basic workout. The lower back is a vital and central point of these motions. Consequently, keeping your lower back in good shape can help you maintain your form and contribute to your total performance.

STANDING WEIGHTED EXTENSION

EQUIPMENT: Barbell
WEIGHT: 25 pounds
SERIES: 3 sets of 15 repetitions

■ Position a barbell comfortably across your shoulders behind your head. Grasp the barbell firmly with both hands.

■ Standing, feet apart, knees bent slightly, bend forward until your torso is parallel to the floor. Keep your head up and your back straight.

■ Return to the upright position. Do not move quickly. Establish a steady flow of motion throughout the exercise.

134

HANGING OBLIQUE FLEX

EQUIPMENT: Chinning bar
SERIES: 100 repetitions; 50 for each side

■ Grasp a chinning bar firmly with both hands and hang with arms at full extension.

■ Twist your body to the right at the waist, creating a flex in the oblique (side) muscle.

■ Turn to the right as far as possible, then reverse and twist to the left.

■ Continue, alternating sides.
Note: The Hanging Oblique Flex is included with this section because the obliques contributed flexibility and support to the lower back.

Abdominals

Exercises for the stomach and sides are included in the basic Body Center Program. However, the abdominal section of your body, in addition to being visually important, requires daily attention to reach and stay in peak condition. Strong stomach muscles aid in the completion of other exercises and help you maintain good posture and physical flexibility. You will find abdominal exercises in every balanced body routine.

KNEE CRUNCH

SERIES: 4 sets of 25 repetitions

■ This exercise is to be used by men whose stomachs are flat.

■ Lie flat on your back on an exercise mat. Intertwine your fingers behind your head.

■ Raise your head, supporting it with your hands, until your chin is on your chest.

■ Keeping your legs and feet together, bring your knees to your chest.

■ With your head in the upright position, extend your legs slightly, keeping your knees bent, and lower your feet to the floor.

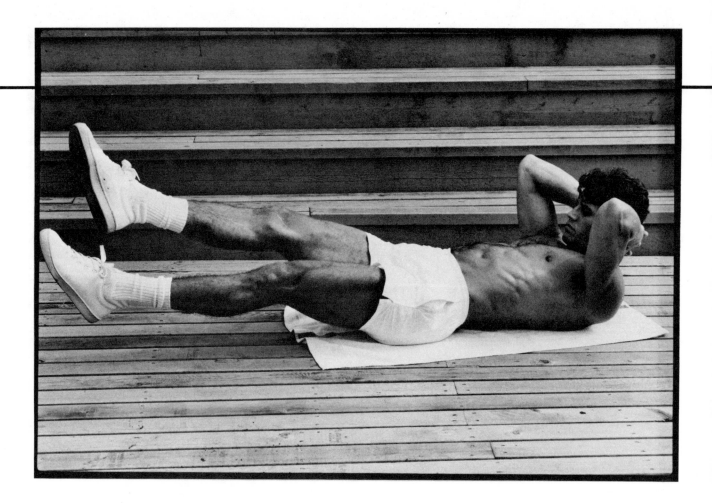

SCISSORS LIFT

SERIES: 4 sets of 25 repetitions

■ This exercise is to be used by men whose stomachs need to be flattened.

■ Lie flat on your back on an exercise mat. Intertwine your fingers behind your head.

■ Raise your head, supporting it with your hands, until your chin is on your chest.

■ Extend your legs straight out in front of you, 6 inches above the floor.

■ Cross one ankle over the other.

■ Lift your legs, alternately crossing your ankles, until you form a right angle with the rest of your body.

■ Lower your legs slowly, repeating the crisscrossing movement.

Neck

There is a controversy concerning exercise movements for the neck area. Many fitness authorities maintain that a strong neck increases the development of your trapezius muscles (the muscle from your neck to your shoulders), along with protecting you from the sagging under your chin that often comes with age. However, some medical authorities dispute this latter claim, holding that any movement in the neck area contributes to the stretching of the skin and thus the loosening of the muscles around the neck, which in turn contributes to sagging under the chin.

FORWARD NECK RAISE

EQUIPMENT: Flat bench, weight plate, towel (optional)
WEIGHT: 5 pounds
SERIES: 50 full-motion repetitions

■ A towel placed between your head and the weight plate can make the exercise more comfortable.

■ Lie flat on your back on a flat bench, head extended over the edge. Place a weight plate behind your head and hold it with both hands.

■ Lower your head as far as possible and then bring your head up, touching your chin to your chest.

■ Repeat the up-and-down movement, reaching full extension and contraction.

BACKWARD NECK RAISE

EQUIPMENT: Flat bench, weight
plate, towel (optional)
WEIGHT: 5 pounds
SERIES: 50 full-motion repetitions

■ A towel placed between your head
and the weight plate can make the exercise more comfortable.

■ Lie on your stomach on a flat bench,
head extended off the edge. Position a
weight plate against the back of your
head and hold it firmly with both
hands.

■ Lower your head completely, as far
as possible, and then bring it back up as
far as possible. Repeat the up-and-
down movement, reaching full extension and contraction.

Wrists

If you used the wrist-formula chart on
page 33, you found that it based your
symmetrical proportions on your wrist
because this was one of the least likely
areas of your body to be influenced by
weight training or weight gain or loss
(unless, of course, these are excessive).
Despite their resistance to building,
there are two very good reasons for
exercising your wrists: (1) Although
your wrists may not noticeably increase
in size, they can increase in strength.
Strong wrists are very important when
handling free-weight equipment. Any
time weight is held in your hand, strong
wrists are vital for support and balance;
(2) wrist exercises build both strength
and *size* on your forearm. This area
between your wrist and your biceps
needs to be developed to create a symmetrical arm. And added strength in
your forearm will support both your
wrist exercises and your upper-arm exercises.

WRIST CURL

EQUIPMENT: Flat bench, dumbbell
WEIGHT: 5 pounds
SERIES: 25 repetitions for each wrist

■ Sit on a flat bench with a dumbbell
before you. With feet flat on the floor,
knees bent, place the back of your right
arm on the top of your right leg, palm
up. Position your arm so that your hand
and lower wrist are extended past your
kneecap.

■ Holding the dumbbell in your right
hand, relax your wrist and let it extend
slowly toward the floor. Keep a good
grip on the weight.

■ Curl your wrist up as far as possible.

Continue the movement, reaching full extension and full contraction.

■ Repeat for your left wrist.

The arm of the wrist being exercised must remain stationary during the exercise. If necessary, you may hold it with your other hand.

WRIST EXTENSION

EQUIPMENT: Flat bench, dumbbell
WEIGHT: 5 pounds
SERIES: 25 repetitions for each wrist

■ Sit on a flat bench with a dumbbell before you. With feet flat on the floor, knees bent, place your right arm, palm down, on your right leg. Position your arm so that your hand and lower wrist are extended past your kneecaps.

■ Grasp the dumbbell firmly in your right hand and relax your right wrist, extending it slowly toward the floor.

■ Curl your wrist up vertically as far as possible. Continue the movement, reaching full extension and contraction.

■ Repeat for your left wrist.

Note: The arm of the wrist being exercised must stay stationary. If necessary, you may hold it with your other hand.

Thirty-Minute, In-Gym Toning Routine

This routine is a straightforward, simple series of movements that works all the major muscle groups without using free weights. This routine is *not* intended as a replacement for your basic workout. Instead, it can be done on alternate days when you feel like going to the gym or on days when your schedule does not allow you the time to complete your full basic in-gym program.

This is not an easy routine; however, it does provide you with a good pump, using only your own body weight. And the toning benefits you derive from this routine are excellent. There are no stretches used in this routine; consequently, the initial warm-up is vital.

WARM-UP

■ Using either an exercise bicycle or a treadmill, begin your warm-up slowly, increasing in speed. Continue for 5 minutes. If neither piece of equipment is available, jog in place, following the same procedure.

Legs and Buttocks

BODY SQUATS

SERIES: 50 repetitions of the full
movement

■ Standing straight, position your feet
shoulder-width apart. Cross your arms
over your chest.

■ Keeping your knees pointed straight
ahead, lower your body as far as possible.

■ Then lift your body up, passing
through the standing position, and onto
your toes.

■ Lower your body and repeat.

Legs

QUAD HOLD

SERIES: 1 movement held 90 seconds

■ Stand approximately 2 feet from a
wall, with your back against the wall.

■ Slowly slide your upper torso down
the wall until you have created a right
angle with your thighs. Your upper

torso should be flat against the wall,
your feet flat on the floor, and your
knees bent. Hold this position.

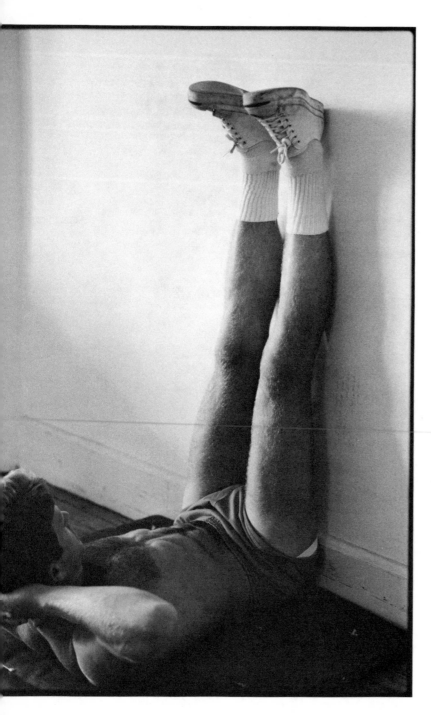

Stomach

PERPENDICULAR 45-DEGREE CRUNCH

SERIES: 50 repetitions

■ This exercise is for men with flat stomachs.

■ Lying on the floor, position your body with your buttocks tight against a wall and your legs extended straight up against the wall.

■ Clasp your hands behind your head, fingers entwined.

■ Raise your head to a 45-degree angle and lower slowly. Be sure to hold in your abdominal muscles.

ABDOMINAL EXTENSION

SERIES: 50 repetitions

■ This exercise is for men with protruding stomachs.

■ Lie flat on your back.

■ Bring your knees up to your chest and wrap your arms around them.

■ Release your knees and extend your legs straight out.

■ Simultaneously, extend your arms over your head to the floor behind you. In the extended position do not allow either your arms or your legs to touch the floor.

■ Stop the movement about 2 inches above the floor.

■ Return to the contracted position, and repeat the movement. Do not touch the floor with your arms and legs between repetitions.

Back

CHINNING BAR PULL-UPS

SERIES: 10 repetitions

■ Grasp a chinning bar firmly with both hands, shoulder-width apart.

■ Let your body hang straight down, arms fully extended.

■ Pull your body up until the bar touches the *back* of your neck.

■ Lower slowly.

Chest

45-DEGREE DIP

EQUIPMENT: Dip stand
SERIES: 10 repetitions

■ Mount a dip stand. Position your hands on the side rails, with your wrists facing out.

■ Raise your body and extend your legs out behind you until your body reaches a 45-degree angle to the floor.

■ Maintain this position and, bending at the elbows, lower your body.

■ Then, raise your body up. Do not reach full extension in the downward movement or full contraction in the upward movement.

■ This exercise is very difficult and should be done carefully.

Shoulders

INVERTED MILITARY PRESS

SERIES: 10 repetitions

■ Do a handstand next to a wall, using the wall for support.

■ Lower your body slowly until your head is almost on the floor, then raise your body up. Do not reach full extension in the upward movement. Until you can manage the balance required for this exercise, a workout partner can hold your legs to keep your body steady.

Biceps

PALMS-IN CHIN-UP

EQUIPMENT: Chinning bar
SERIES: 10 repetitions

■ Grasp a chinning bar firmly with both hands, palms in, shoulder-width apart.

■ Let your body hang straight down, arms fully extended.

■ Raise your body until the bar is under your chin.

■ Slowly lower your body back to the extended position.

Triceps

PALMS-OUT CHIN-UP

EQUIPMENT: Chinning bar
SERIES: 10 repetitions

■ Grasp a chinning bar firmly with both hands, palms out, shoulder-width apart.

■ Let your body hang straight down, arms fully extended.

■ Raise your body until the bar is under your chin.

■ Slowly lower your body back to the extended position.

COOL DOWN

■ Jog in place, beginning slowly and increasing your speed. Continue for 10 minutes, then gradually begin to slacken your pace. When you reach the level of a fast walk, begin to move around the gym. Shake out your legs and arms. Slow down more until you are at a normal walking pace. Continue moving, and bend, stretch, lift, and breathe, releasing your body.

At-Home Routine

The Body Center recognizes that not all men are interested in making a commitment to either a gym membership or an orchestrated exercise program. Consequently, the at-home workout is designed to involve all the muscle groups in an uncomplicated toning and firming routine.

This series of exercises was not created to build or sculpt your physique, but, instead, to increase your dexterity, promote strength in your muscles, and add tone and firmness to your body.

The routine takes 30 minutes to complete and can be done every day, if you wish. However, you can accomplish results with three workouts a week, on alternate days.

Use light weights. The dumbbells required in this series of exercises are used essentially to establish form, add resistance and maintain muscle tautness. Heavy weights are not necessary and can be dangerous when you are working out alone. Also, the workout is a consecutive series of movements with many repetitions and only 30-second rest periods between exercises. In only one exercise in the workout do you release the dumbbells. Consequently, light weights, 5 to 10 pounds, are more functional than heavy weights for this routine. In addition, the weights should always be light enough for you to handle comfortably and manipulate safely.

The only equipment you will need for the workout is 2 dumbbells, a mirror, weight plate, and exercise mat. Adjustable weights are helpful but not required.

Do the routine with a steady rhythm. Do not rush through the exercises, but do not do them so slowly that you lose your momentum.

Never release the weights unless specifically instructed to do so.

Take only 30-second rest periods between exercises.

If you are using adjustable weights, make sure that the collars are firmly in place.

For men completing the basic in-gym program, the at-home workout can be a productive alternative routine for maintaining strength and dexterity on days when you are unable to get to your health club.

WARM-UP

JUMPING JACKS

SERIES: 100 repetitions (At first you may want to divide this number of repetitions into 2 or even 4 sets of either 50 or 25 each. If you do so, rest only 30 seconds between each set.)

■ Holding a dumbbell in each hand, complete the full range of movement.

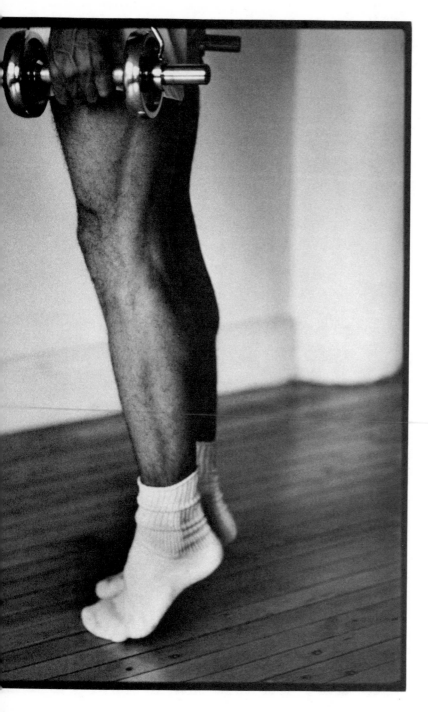

Calves

CALF FLEX

EQUIPMENT: 2 dumbbells, mirror, exercise mat
WEIGHT: 5 to 10 pounds for each dumbbell
SERIES: 50 repetitions

■ Standing, feet flat on the floor and holding a dumbbell in each hand, arms fully extended at your sides, lift your body onto your toes.

■ Return to the flatfooted position.

Thighs

LUNGE

EQUIPMENT: 2 dumbbells, mirror, exercise mat
WEIGHT: 5 to 10 pounds for each dumbbell
SERIES: 25 repetitions for each leg, alternating legs

■ Standing straight with a dumbbell in each hand, arms fully extended at your sides, step out with your left leg as far as possible. Your right leg should be almost parallel to the floor with the heel raised to accommodate the stretch.

■ Return your left leg to starting position and step out with your right leg.

■ Repeat the movement.

Buttocks

PELVIC THRUST

EQUIPMENT: dumbbell or weight
plate, mirror, exercise mat
WEIGHT: 5 to 10 pounds
SERIES: 25 repetitions

■ This is the only movement in which
you do not hold the weight.

■ Lie flat on your back. Spread your
legs and bend your knees, placing your
feet flat on the floor.

■ Rest your upper body on the back of
your shoulders. Place a weight plate on
your diaphragm.

■ Thrust your pelvic area up as high
as possible, clenching your buttocks on
the thrust.

■ Lower the pelvis down and release
your buttocks, but do not reach the
floor on the downward movement. If
you use a dumbbell instead of a weight
plate, position it carefully and watch
your balance.

Stomach

ABDOMINAL EXTENSION

EQUIPMENT: 2 dumbbells, mirror, exercise mat

SERIES: 50 repetitions (You may want to do this exercise in 2 sets of 25 repetitions. If so, rest only 30 seconds between sets.)

■ Holding a dumbbell in each hand, lie flat on your back.

■ Bring your knees up to your chest. Position your arms in front of you, with your wrists touching your kneecaps.

■ In one motion, extend your arms straight up and over your head, reaching behind you, as you extend your legs straight out. In the fully extended position your legs and arms are both directly above the floor. However, do not allow them to touch the floor.

■ Stop the movement just above resolution, and contract your knees and arms again, returning to the starting position.

Sides

ALTERNATING SIDE BENDS

EQUIPMENT: 2 dumbbells, mirror, exercise mat
WEIGHT: 5 to 10 pounds for each dumbbell
SERIES: 25 repetitions for each side

■ Standing straight, hold a dumbbell in each hand, arms fully extended, positioned approximately 6 inches from your sides.

■ Keeping your shoulders straight, alternately bend to each side. Do not accomplish the bend with your shoulders; rather, your oblique muscles must feel the action of the movement.

Back

BENT-OVER ROWING

EQUIPMENT: 2 dumbbells, mirror, exercise mat
WEIGHT: 5 to 10 pounds for each dumbbell
SERIES: 25 repetitions

■ Standing with a dumbbell in each hand, bend over, forming a right angle.

■ Keeping your back straight and holding your head up, position your elbows away from your body. Raise and lower both dumbbells simultaneously. As the weights are brought up, they should fit snugly into your armpits, then reach full extension toward the floor.

Chest

LATERAL FLYS

EQUIPMENT: 2 dumbbells, mirror, exercise mat
WEIGHT: 5 to 10 pounds for each dumbbell
SERIES: 25 repetitions

■ Lie flat on the floor, arms fully extended on the floor perpendicular to your body.

■ Grasping a dumbbell in each hand and bending your arms slightly at the elbows, raise your arms simultaneously toward the center of your body. Keep the motion in and above your chest.

■ Lower your arms back to the sides, keeping your elbows slightly bent. Stop the downward motion when your elbows touch the floor.

Shoulders

ALTERNATING RAISE

EQUIPMENT: 2 dumbbells, mirror, exercise mat
WEIGHT: 5 to 10 pounds for each dumbbell
SERIES: 25 repetitions for each shoulder

■ Stand, holding a dumbbell in each hand on either side of your face, palms in.

■ Keeping the dumbbells close throughout the exercise, extend your arms, alternately, straight up, reaching full extension, then lower them to starting position.

Biceps

ALTERNATING CURLS

EQUIPMENT: 2 dumbbells, mirror, exercise mat

WEIGHT: 5 to 10 pounds for each dumbbell

SERIES: 25 repetitions for each arm

■ Stand, holding a dumbbell in each hand. Position your elbows firmly against your sides near your hip bones. Rest your hands, palms up, on your thighs.

■ Alternately raise the dumbbells, keeping your elbows tightly in position, to full contraction and then return them to your thighs.

Triceps

ALTERNATING KICKBACK

EQUIPMENT: 2 dumbbells, mirror, exercise mat
WEIGHT: 5 to 10 pounds for each dumbbell
SERIES: 25 repetitions for each arm

■ Grasp a dumbbell in each hand.

■ Standing, bend over until your torso is parallel to the floor.

■ Position your elbows tight against your sides.

■ Keeping your head up and your elbows stationary, extend your hands alternately out behind you. Do not guide the motion straight back. The extension should be directed back and *away* from the body as far as your secure elbows will allow.

■ Return your hands to the original position after each extension.

COOL DOWN
WALK

■ For 5 minutes after you have completed your routine, move around the exercise area, stretching, bending. Breathe deeply.

Vacation Fitness Routine

Very few men want to consider exercise when they go on vacation. Leaving the stress and strain of everyday life usually includes leaving your commitment to fitness. The Body Center does not suggest that you travel with a full set of weights and your workout chart.

If you are contemplating an extended trip, you might investigate the possibility of reciprocal agreements between your fitness facility and those in other areas or cities. A Body Center membership is good at all their clubs and some other gyms as well. And many other clubs have similar arrangements with facilities in other parts of the country. Some gyms even have affiliates in Europe.

If you are planning a short trip or holiday, it is not necessary to attempt to maintain your complete workout pro-

gram. In fact, some authorities suggest periodically taking off a week from a regular routine to give your body a chance to rest and revitalize. This does not mean that you should take off one week out of every four, but a week away from the gym every three or four months cannot do you any harm and might even be beneficial.

Exercise on vacation should not be an onerous duty, but an attribute of your vacation—a method by which you can enjoy your holiday to the fullest.

The exercises suggested for you to complete on your vacation are for two purposes: (1) After a hard in-gym program, it is a good idea to do some movements to keep your body from getting stiff; and (2) the movements are designed to keep you limber and supple so you can enjoy your vacation.

Vacation sports can be an exciting and adventurous aspect of your holiday. Swimming, boating, running on a beach, playing water polo, climbing a mountain, playing tennis, and so forth, are all great exercises that can help tone your body and add strength to your muscles—which, incidentally, may be helpful when you return to the gym.

If you have fulfilled your commitment to your regular routine, you should be able to handle new and different sports experiences. However, be aware that some sports use muscles differently from the way you have been training, so, just as with any new physical endeavor, you should start slowly. Use the vacation fitness routine to aid you in staying limber and keeping you ready to go.

The routine is a simple series of stretch-calisthenic movements, requiring no special equipment and taking only a few moments to complete.

Do the following exercises in the morning, before breakfast, each day of your vacation.

Calves

■ Stand approximately 3 feet from a column or wall, facing the support.

■ Lean forward and support your body with your forearms.

■ Bring one leg 2 feet forward. The leg in the forward position should be directly under your shoulder. The back leg should be behind your body.

■ Bend your forward leg slightly and push off your rear leg, keeping the toes of both feet in place.

■ Raise and lower the heel of your back foot slowly, creating a stretch in the calf.

■ Repeat the movement several times.

■ Switch leg positions and repeat.

Thighs/Hamstrings/ Lower Back

■ Stand next to any waist-high object (a table or desk is best).

■ Lift one leg and place it fully extended on top of the support. Bending from the waist, reach for the ankle of the elevated leg.

■ Grasp the ankle firmly and hold the position for 30 seconds.

■ Release and return your upper body to the upright position, leaving the leg elevated.

■ Repeat the movement.

■ Switch legs and complete the movement twice for your other leg.

Hips/Buttocks/ Inner Thighs

■ Position your body on your knees and hands.

■ Lift one leg out to the side and then extend it straight back out behind you. Hold for 30 seconds.

■ Release and return your leg to the original position.

■ Bending your knee, bring your leg in under your body, positioning your knee to your chest. Hold for 30 seconds.

■ Release and return your leg to the original position.

■ Repeat the sequence again with the same leg.

■ Complete the movement twice for your other leg.

Lower Back/Legs/ Arms/Shoulders

■ Lie flat on your back. Extend your arms out behind your head.

■ Bring your legs up, keeping them straight, until you create a right angle with your body.

■ At the same time, raise your arms from the shoulders, meeting your legs at a center point over your body.

■ Grasp your ankles. Hold for 30 seconds.

■ Release and return to the original position.

■ Repeat the movement.

Stomach/Lower Back/ Shoulders

■ Lie flat on your back.

■ Bring your knees up to your chest and wrap your arms around them. Hold for 30 seconds.

■ Release your knees and extend your legs straight out and down.

■ Simultaneously, extend your arms over your head to the floor behind you. In the extended position do not allow either your arms or your legs to touch the floor.

■ Stop the movement about 2 inches above the floor and hold for 30 seconds.

■ Return to the contracted position, and repeat the movement. Do not touch the floor with your arms and legs between repetitions.

Office Antistress Routine

Virtually every man has experienced a stressful and tense workday. And the strain can show in your body.

Aware of the importance of fitness, many companies have organized exercise facilities in their office buildings. This is a valuable and important innovation. But not all offices have gyms; and even if yours does have one there may not always be time to take full advantage of it.

If you spend your lunchtime at the gym doing your regular Body Center Program, chances are you do not suffer from the normal tightening and tensing of your muscles that afflicts many executives. But if you do not break your workday with exercise, preferring to do your workout before or after your job, you may feel the pressures of your work in your body.

It is obviously difficult to exercise in a business suit, and the Body Center office antistress routine is not designed to actually give you a workout. Instead, it is a series of movements that will help relieve the tightness that often reflects the stress of your job.

The routine is done either at or near your desk. No special equipment is required and the routine can be completed in 10 minutes. The next time you feel the strain of work settling in your muscles, take a few minutes and complete the routine.

SUSTAINED NECK FLEX

■ Sitting at your desk, lower your head straight down until your face is almost to the top of the desk.

■ Clasp your hands behind your neck. Lift your head up from the desk as you pull forward with your hands. Keep your elbows out as far as possible.

■ When your head reaches the straight-up position, increase the pressure with your hands, equalizing it by pushing back harder with your head.

■ Hold the equalized position for 30 seconds and gently release.

■ Repeat the movements.

SEATED DIP

■ Sit straight in a desk chair that has arms.

■ Position one hand firmly on each arm of the chair and extend your legs straight out in front of you.

■ Lift your body up from the chair using only your arms.

■ Reach the fully extended position and hold for 30 seconds.

■ Release and slowly lower your body down to the chair.

■ Repeat the movement.

TRUNK TWIST

SERIES: 10 repetitions for each side

■ Stand straight and clasp your hands behind your head.

■ Twist your body side-to-side from the hips. Keep your elbows out and really push against each side.

SUSTAINED BACK FLEX

SERIES: 2 repetitions

■ Stand behind your desk.

■ Lean over from the waist and grasp the far edge of the desk firmly with both hands. Your arms should be fully extended. Do not bend your elbows. If your desk is narrow, move your lower body back away from the edge.

■ Keeping your feet flat and legs firmly in place, pull toward your body with your hands. Hold the pull position for 30 seconds and release.

■ Repeat the movement twice.

ARM SWING

SERIES: 1 minute for each movement

■ Standing, extend your arms straight out to the sides, forming a right angle on each side of your body.

■ Beginning the movement in the forward direction, make small circles with your arms, widening the arcs slowly for 1 minute, until your arms are creating very wide circles.

■ Reverse your arms at your widest arc and continue the movement, slowly decreasing the size of the circles for 1 minute until you have returned to your original position.

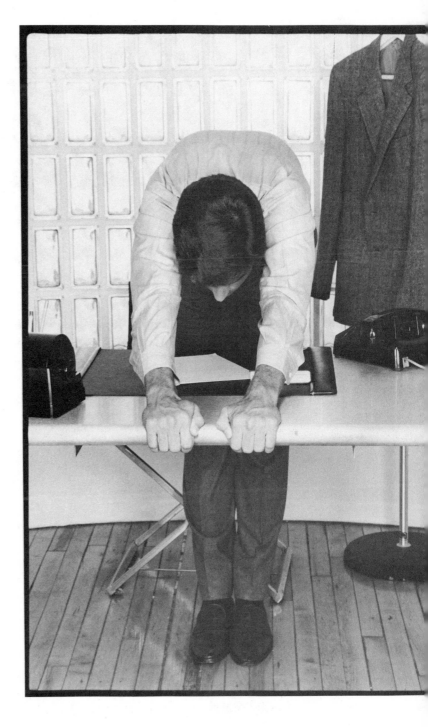

Ten-Minute Strength Routine

Isometric exercise has been a part of the fitness world for many years. The Body Center has adapted a selection of these movements for your program for two reasons: (1) Isometrics have been proven to build strength, and (2) isometrics are easy to do and can be completed at virtually any time or place.

Isometrics are exercises in which you build strength through resistance, pitting one muscle against another, or your muscle against an immovable object.

The rapidity with which you can complete an isometric exercise is not only a positive factor in terms of simplicity and ease of accomplishment, but a necessity in terms of completing the movement properly. Individual isometric exercises should not be held for more than a few seconds. Additional time will not extend the effectiveness of the exercise and can result in sore muscles.

Because of the nature of isometric exercises, the position possibilities appear to be endless. However, for your use, the Body Center has adapted and created moves that reinforce not only the muscle groups trained in the basic in-gym program but also the area of each of the individual muscles that is most likely to be placed in a stressful position during your basic workout. The added strength offered by isometric exercise will then add to your in-gym program in two ways: strength of the overall muscle, and support of the muscle's stress area.

The entire isometric routine should be done twice, with a 5-minute rest between the two series.

Isometrics can be done every day, but it is not necessary to do them that often. They are the most beneficial to your in-gym workout if they are done the day before you plan to do your basic routine.

These exercises can be done in your office, on a plane, riding in a car, or even sitting in a movie.

Calves

SEATED RAISE

■ Sit normally, feet flat on the floor. Rest your forearms on your thighs.

■ Press down with your body weight on your forearms as you raise the heels of your feet.

■ Hold for 5 seconds.

Thighs

LEG EXTENSION

■ Seated, place your feet under an immovable object, 6 inches or more from the floor (the seat in front of you on an airplane is ideal).

■ Lift your feet straight up, pulling against the object.

■ Hold for 5 seconds.

Buttocks

CLENCH

■ Seated or standing, clench and tighten your buttocks muscles together.

■ Hold for 5 seconds.

Stomach

ABBREVIATED CRUNCH

■ Seated, place your legs together.

■ Raise your feet 6 inches from the floor, using your abdominal muscles. Make sure it is the stomach muscles that do the lifting.

■ Hold for 5 seconds.

Back

PULL-UP

■ Seated, with your feet flat on the floor, place your hands under your feet, palms up.

■ Keeping your feet stationary, pull from your hands, creating a resistance in your latissimus muscles.

■ Hold for 5 seconds.

Chest

PRESS

- Stand facing a wall. Cross your arms at chest level.

- Lean your forearms against the wall and push.

- Hold for 5 seconds.

Shoulders

LATERAL RAISE

■ Seated, position your right arm, elbow bent laterally, in front of your body, chest high.

■ Rest your left hand on your right arm.

■ Push down on your right arm with your left hand as you lift your right arm.

■ Switch arms and repeat movement for your left shoulder.

■ Hold for 5 seconds on each side.

Biceps

EXTENSION

■ Seated or standing, position your right arm in the half-contracted curl position.

■ Grasp your right hand with your left hand, palms together, left hand on top.

■ Press down with your left hand as you contract your right arm.

■ Switch positions and repeat the movement for your left arm.

■ Hold each position for 5 seconds.

Triceps

EXTENSION

■ Seated or standing, position your right arm in the half-contracted curl position.

■ Grasp the top of your right hand with the palm of your left hand.

■ Push up with your left hand as you lower your right arm.

■ Switch positions and repeat the movement for your left arm.

■ Hold each position for 5 seconds.

WAIT 5 MINUTES AND REPEAT THE COMPLETE ISOMETRIC SERIES.

chapter seven

NUTRITION AND DIET

Nutrition and diet discussions are rapidly becoming taboo subjects at cocktail parties along with religion and politics. Almost everyone has his own ideas, usually "medically proven," about the proper use of vitamin and mineral supplements and the most effective and latest diet craze.

There are a few basic facts about nutrition and diet that every man should know; and anyone involved in a serious and strenuous fitness routine should certainly be cognizant of his own body's nutritional needs. But along with what to eat, *when* to eat is also important.

Carbohydrates

Obviously, dietary requirements, particularly for men involved in a workout program, can vary from individual to individual. These needs are largely based on personal physical growth and the extent of individual activity. However, the one requirement that everyone has when working out is *energy.*

Complex carbohydrates are the most efficient source of energy when you are exercising at maximum level. Foods such as pasta, whole-grain bread, and fruit are absorbed relatively slowly and stimulate the production of insulin over a longer period of time. Insulin increases the production of glycogen in the liver and muscles, which is essential for muscular contractions.

Fats

Foods containing a high percentage of fats are not good before your workout. These foods delay gastric emptying, thus directing your blood supply away from the exercise process and concentrating it on your digestion.

Protein

It is not a good idea to eat high-protein foods before exercising. Like fats, these foods also require extra effort to digest. Protein and fatty foods should be eaten after you have finished your routine. *Excess protein is not necessary to produce muscle tissue.* The recommended amount of protein for a man doing heavy training is 1 to 2 grams per kilogram of body weight, and 0.8 grams of protein to 1 kilogram of body weight for a man not involved in a heavy training program (1 kilogram equals 2.2 pounds).

Protein has become a panacea for many bodybuilders. However, excess protein has not been proven to increase muscular stamina or development. In fact, it can actually encourage other problems. Excess protein can cause an increase in water loss due to increased urination. This water loss can cause the washing away of valuable minerals, vitamins, and body enzymes.

Mealtime

The scheduling of your meals either before or after your workout is basically an individual preference. Some men will find that they will accomplish more in their routine if they eat a banana or other small snack a short time before their exercise. Others may want to have a larger meal an hour or so before beginning their workout. After your exercise program is over, you may find that the workout has taken the edge off your appetite; or you may have an immediate need to replace some of the energy you have expended in your routine. It is a good idea to experiment and discover which eating methods provide you with the most positive results.

Vitamins

Although there is *no scientific evidence* to indicate that taking vitamins above the basic requirements has any benefit, it is important that, as you exercise, you make sure your diet includes foods high in thiamine, riboflavin, and niacin. Although the normal vitamin requirements are met with a good, healthy diet, the need for these specific vitamins is increased simultaneously with the increased expenditure of energy when you work out. Your additional body requirements for these vitamins can be met by including foods high in these vitamins in your diet, such as complex carbohydrates like whole grains and cereals.

Minerals

Minerals can be of more concern. Sweating, water loss in the steam room or sauna, or water loss due to a misguided intake of excess protein often results in the depletion of the body's stores of sodium, potassium, calcium, magnesium, and various other trace minerals. Most of this mineral loss does not present a problem to the normally healthy individual, as the minerals can be rapidly restored with the proper foods. Sodium, for instance, is rarely a problem in our salt-consuming population, and calcium is rarely a difficulty unless the individual is on a high-protein, low-carbohydrate diet. But potassium can be a major concern. *Potassium is a vital ingredient* in your energy and strength levels, and it is easily lost through sweating as you exercise. Eating food high in this valuable mineral is very important when you are exercising. Bananas and nuts are among the high-potassium foods.

Your Basic Diet

Diet and nutrition, like your exercise program itself, is largely a matter of common sense and the avoidance of fad or miracle eating programs.

There are no vitamins or minerals that are helpful in building muscle beyond the normal level. Excess protein does not cause increased muscle bulk. There are no miracle foods that will cause you to develop a superbody overnight—despite advertisements to the contrary.

A simple, basic diet that includes protein from fish and poultry, whole-grain cereals and breads, fresh vegetables and fruits, an adequate, but not overindulgent amount of fats, contributes to balanced nutrition and your balanced body.

Weight Control

Weight control is a concern for approximately 40 million Americans. And just as there are no miracle foods that will provide you with a super-body overnight, there are no miracle foods that will remove excess weight with little or no effort.

The Body Center Program maintains that a good weight-loss program includes all the basic nutritionally required foods, in limited quantities. However, the selection of your diet should be a decision between you and your doctor. Nevertheless, it is important to take your exercise program into consideration when you plan your diet.

Many men embarking on an exercise program do so because they are overweight and hope that the workouts will trim down their excess poundage. It is, however, vital to realize that *exercise alone will not accomplish weight-loss goals.* Diet is mandatory. By the same token, it has been proven that for a weight-control program to have long-lasting or continuing results, an accompanying program

of intense exercise is necessary. Thus diet and exercise work together to help attain weight-loss goals.

The influence of exercise on your weight-control program is twofold. Although the amount of energy expended during *any* routine becomes nebulous when the actual calorie-use count is totaled (walking a city block at a normal pace uses only one calorie), the action in the exercise process speeds up your metabolism and encourages your use of calories, thus aiding in the weight-loss process. In addition, as you train and tone your muscles, your positive emotional state will enable you to better follow your weight-loss plan.

One of the most difficult aspects of any exercise program or diet is *staying with it,* particularly at the beginning, before the first results appear and give encouragement to you. The following is a series of suggestions aimed toward keeping you on your diet and adjusting your eating habits so that you can keep the excess poundage off.

DIETING TIPS

1. Eat slowly. It has been ascertained that slender individuals eat slowly, while overweight people often gulp down their food.

2. Eat in one place. Select a location in your home as the spot for your meals and have them there regularly. Do not wander about your home with food in your hand.

3. Put utensils down between bites. Holding your utensils throughout your meal encourages you to eat faster.

4. Do not adorn your food. It is not necessary for food to look good to provide you with your required nutrition. In fact, the simpler your meals, the better. The more attractive your food, the more you are enticed to eat.

5. Make a list of acceptable foods. Carry this list with you on all shopping trips and buy *only* the items that are included. Do not be led astray by bargains on foods that are not on your list. They may be less expensive to buy, but they will cost more on your figure.

6. Do not do anything else as you eat. If in the past you have enjoyed your dinner while watching television or reading a book, set aside these activities and concentrate on your food. If you are distracted while you eat, you might finish more food than you should.

THE FUTURE

It is interesting to note that many of the terms used in fitness or self-improvement routines are also applicable to creating works of art: form, proportion, sculpting, symmetry. And, in some ways, as a man exercises and develops his body, he is creating his own artistic statement.

There is a basic and fundamental difference, however, between creating a work of art and developing your body to its peak potential. Your body is never finished. It is not possible to put aside the tools of your achievement and go on to the next project. Maintaining your body in its peak condition is a constant and ongoing process.

The philosophy of the Body Center Program as stated in the beginning of this book is to place physical exercise in its proper perspective within the rest of your life. You have already made your decision to exercise. Remember, it is your body that you are working with. Treat it with respect, affection, and discipline, and it will respond with vitality, good looks, and support for your other endeavors.

ACKNOWLEDGMENTS

The production of *Balanced Body* could not have been accomplished without the professional expertise and valuable contributions of Roslyn Siegel, book editor; Ken Sansone, art director; Joyce Romano, photographic production coordinator; Herbert Walker, M.D., Steven Herman, M.D., Daniel Sikowitz, M.S., Philip Migliarese, Jr., M.S., medical advisors; Keith Peterson, illustrator; Reinhold Siegal, photography assistant; David Parker, grooming assistant; James Webster, nautical advisor; John Rhode, the Body Center; Pieter O'Brien, Henry Grethel, Inc.; Tom Laspina, The Artists and Models Group; Jan Gonet, Elite Modeling Agency; Tom Harvey, L'Image Model Management, Inc.; Mystique Model Management; Roseanne Vecchione and Dan Deeley, Wilhelmina Models, Inc.; Vicky Pribble and Barbara Lantz, Zoli Models, Inc.; the Islander's Club; and the models: Robert Brofman, pp. 66, 67, 68, 69, 70; Michael Cavanaugh, pp. 57, 58, 59, 84, 85, 86, 87, 89; Drew Coburn, pp. 36, 43, 162, 165, 174, 175, 184; Carter Collins, pp. 164, 173, 184, 186; John Curley, pp. 50, 51, 52, 53; Dennis Decker, pp. 48, 118, 119; Jerry Dinome, pp. 46, 108, 109, 110, 111, 112, 113, 114, 115; Bob Gill, pp. 126, 141, 142, 144, 145, 146; Jonathon Harris, pp. 8, 184; Owen Hartley, p. 176; Bruce Hulse, pp. 2, 14, 149, 150, 151, 152, 153, 154, 155, 156, 157, 158, 159; Jiles Kirkland, pp. 24, 120, 124; Charles Mandracchia, pp. 54, 62, 64, 72, 82, 90, 98, 106; George Paterson, pp. 92, 93, 94, 96; Jay Paul, pp. 100, 101, 103, 104, 105; Brian Terrell, pp. 74, 75, 76, 77, 78, 79, 80, 81; Steven Thomas, pp. 56, 60, 61, 63, 167, 168, 169; Richard Villella, pp. 7, 13, 18, 133, 135, 136, 137, 139, 160, with Charlotte, p. 176; Charles Winslow, jacket, pp. 116, 172.

The author is personally grateful for the help and encouragement of Harry Trumbore, David Napoli, Roger Sharp, Ken Kendricks, Ken Haak, Jack Haber, Damaris Rowland, Barry Van Lenten, Carol Fein, Syd Kahn, Helen Berkowitz, John Whyte, John Robinson, Gil Johnson, Bill Roberts, Terry Lee, Merrill Sindler, Chip Lopez, Nina Blanchard, and William Pitt, III. Special thanks to Harvey Klinger and William Buckingham for their constant and remarkable support and patience.